ISBN 978-0-428-78413-3
PIBN 10814667

DESPITE THE WORLD:

A new Romantic Play,

IN TWO PARTS AND FOUR TABLEAUX.

BY

THE HON. LEWIS WINGFIELD

AND

GENEVIEVE DE GUERBEL.

PART I. BERLIN AND SANS SOUCI, 1746.

PART II. VERSAILLES AND PARIS, 1751.

For certain Portions of the Plot the Author is indebted to an Italian Work.

Dramatis Personæ.

——◆——

THECLA, COUNTESS VON THÜRENAU.

OLIVIA, PRINCESS OF NOVGOROD (her Sister).

DUCHESS OF VALENCE.

MADAME DE PIERREFITTE.

FREDERICK THE SECOND OF PRUSSIA.

MONSIEUR DE VOLTAIRE.

COUNT JULIAN OF TOLEDO.

PRINCE OF NOVGOROD.

BARON ERFÜRT.

LAROQUE.

DR. MARTIN.

DESPITE THE WORLD.

PART I.

TABLEAU I.—*Drawing-room in Thecla's castle. Doors* R. *and* L. *In* C. *in flat an arch, with a thin curtain down, opening down the centre.*

THECLA *and* LAROQUE. *She seated by a table, he standing over her, a paper in his hand.*

THECLA. Thank you, good Laroque. Your ode is graceful, and, as it should be, eminently flattering. You are a born poet.

LAROQUE. And you, Countess, a born queen, fit sovereign for His Gracious Majesty King Frederick's intellectual Court. As for the poor ode, madam, you were ever too indulgent to my humble worth.

THEC. Take care! that is another of the thousand falsehoods which you propound daily for my benefit. I am not indulgent; never was; and never intend to be. My love of frankness, my worship of Truth at any price, reaches possibly the verge of madness. It is a folly which in this lying world whereon we feebly strive will doubtless meet with proper punishment, for, after all, society has a right to be deceived. Yet I am bold enough to cling to the opinions formed on my own theories. Do I ever blame the world for the slime which now and then it seeks to cast at me? No, my heart is brave; I meet its slanders with contempt.

LAR. Slander to you, the beautiful widow? So witty, rich, adored? Chosen to sit on an ideal throne; ruling a kingdom whose chief wealth is intellect.

THEC. All the more cause for slander, friend Laroque, where coins of wit are the chief currency. The world accepts idols on the sole condition of breaking them at will, and I for one see no cause for blame. The world and I are excellent friends, jogging quietly side by side together, wreathing one another's locks with drooping blossoms day by day, and waving the vase of incense in the air, the more effectually to blind each other. By the way, that epigram you turned on me last night was really vastly clever, for it sent a smile round all the lips at Court.

P

LAR. I turn an epigram at your expense. Oh, Countess, believe me!——

THEO. Come, come, Laroque. Down on your knees and confess at once. Admit that the very paper in your hand in which I am likened to Juno and Venus and Minerva, all in one, will, ere yonder sun be set, have been applied to every swan-like neck and marble brow in town!

LAR. I will admit no such thing. I solemnly protest that in your presence I could not flatter even if I would.

THEO. (*with a sigh of satisfaction*). Thank you. A new kind of compliment, and most refreshing. While I think of it, you have never told me the price of that delectable composition. One must pay for admittance to Olympus. What does it cost to stand in Juno's car? What does Venus ask? (*declaiming, pompously*). "To veil her eyes with tawny hair in shame?" Ha! Ha! I have it. The place is vacant, and you would fain shade your noble brow under the Poet Laureate's crown. Is it not so?

LAR. Countess, you are all goodness!

THEO. Well. His Majesty will be here to-day—or rather Count Hecksen—for our monarch is not above masquerade, and wishes his incognito to be respected. I will speak a word for you—no thanks. And now—Presto! change. Drop the poet and resume the secretary, the more useful if not the less ornamental of the two. What letters have we here to-day?

LAR. Here is one from the great philosopher, the Abbé des Fontaines.

THEO. Read.

LAR. " Divine Glicera. The gout and my creditors combined keep me to my room. Being very miserable, I would banish care, and therefore write to you——"

THEO. No more nonsense. Sends he no news?

LAR. A long postscript.

THEO. Read it.

LAR. "You are fond of oddities. Seek out and study one but recently arrived at Frederick's Court. A gentleman, half poet, half philosopher, attached to the Spanish Embassy; a woman-hater, who denies the existence of the butterfly god, believes in all that we deny, and disbelieves our common articles of faith, such, for example, my queen, as your irresistible powers to charm. The bear is named Count Julian of Toledo. Muzzle him. Read his grand tragedy called 'Sappho.' I have seen worse. I can bear my gout no more. Adieu."

THEO. Invite him here at once (*writes*). Nay, take this note with your own hand. What else?

LAR. A letter from Garrick.

THEO. (*snatching it*). From Garrick! Give it to me quickly

(*reads*). "You ask news of me. I can but repeat what I said in London, when we stood together on the dismantled stage, amid the ruins of Hamlet's cardboard palace. Each night as I remove the paint from my face I scrutinize the lines which death's finger is slowly but surely weaving there, and muse upon my fate. There is yet time. If I so willed it, I could yet erase those awful prints. But 'twixt life and art I have made my choice, and shall, like Molière, die an actor on the boards." (*She remains buried in thought.*) Poor Garrick! His life of shadows is perhaps the true life after all! Any more letters?

LAR. One from the Duke of Liera.

THEC. To the flames.

LAR. Without reading it?

THEC. I know what it contains.

LAR. From Count Heilbach.

THEC. To the flames. That makes his twenty-third.

LAR. Verses—verses—verses. Enough to paper a room.

THEC. To the flames.

LAR. A petition from a poor family. That to the flames, too?

THEC. No. Hold! Give it to me. Write,—" Good for 700 florins, payable annually, on presentation of this order."

LAR. Another note—a strange one this. Only one word—a name—Voltaire.

THEC. (*rising suddenly*). Voltaire at Berlin! So suddenly, without so much as a message!

[*Page announces at door,* " M. de Voltaire."

THEC. Admit him at once. Don't go, Laroque.

[LAROQUE *sits at table.*

Enter VOLTAIRE.

(*Taking both* VOLTAIRE'S *hands in hers*). Now this is kind! When did you arrive, and why?*

VOL. Thecla, my child, I arrived but yesterday. Mahomet turned me out of France.

THEO. How?

VOL. Not the man, the work penned by your humble servant. It is quite surprising what a hubbub was raised by those few poor halting lines. I laughed awhile, and then I withdrew Mahomet. He and I, Atheist and Mussulman, travelled trgether in a royal coach. A mustachioed grenadier galloped at either door. On the road, I converted one gentleman to my peculiar code of thought, and filled the other's skin with wine—ruined them both for life, poor men. No matter. Here I am, safe and sound, and so is Mahomet. Once a poet, always a philosopher, I have come to try my hand at a new trade. Behold in me an ambassador, clad in the panoply of a mysterious mission.

* The two must stand all through this scene.

THEC. You!

VOL. Yes.   Everybody is an ambassador now-a-days.

THEC. From whom?

VOL. I play, you see, a double part; one burlesque, the other sentimental—ambassador and outlaw. I have come from myself, to induce Frederick to take up arms in my behalf. I began by imploring him to do nothing of the kind—the best way of gaining my point, although he's not a woman.

THEC. And what said the king?

VOL. As usual, a multitude of sonorous words, very excellent in themselves, but meaningless as strung by him. Heigho! I am already weary of the many-sided character I am called upon to play. As a literary man, I have been pelted with eulogistic verses by every fool in Prussia who can read and write, all of whom unite to wave in my face the many-coloured rag which men call glory. I assured them earnestly that I am a great man, and they believed it. As a philosopher, I had gravely to receive a stupendous deputation of elderly orang-outangs, who appear to consider philosophy incompatible with common-sense. As an outlaw, I'm pursued by all the ragamuffins in the town, who vie with one another which shall first dip into my purse. And so, like a worried animal, I come, harassed and panting, to you, imploring only rest, and for a brief space to be forgotten. May I crave that, as you are an angel—happily minus the fiery sword—you will open to me the gates of your earthly paradise?

THEC. A poor paradise, Voltaire; for in it is but a weak semblance of the Tree of Life, without its twin sister, the Tree of Happiness. A paltry Eden, wherein all glitters with the tinsel of the stage.

VOL. My enthusiastic Thecla! You were not wont to speak thus. A change seems——

THEC. Dear friend, are we not all for ever changing, and does not each revolving year whisper its own counsel ere it vanishes? I cannot but feel that it is a terrible fate to stand over the abyss of one's illusions, seeking to trace something tangible in its uncertain depths.

VOL. Do its chasms yawn less awfully than the bitter gulf of doubt over which it is my lot to hover? Depend upon it, grandfather Adam was wrong, whose chief legacy was a feverish desire for search into hidden things. Ignorance is true happiness; one little dose of opium, and a long sound sleep, without a waking.

THEC. If you choose opium, I have my philtre, too. I have distilled into a golden draught every sparkling pleasure which our frivolous, feeble, sceptical age affords, and quaff it daily, till rendered sick and dizzy by satiety.

VOL. Double the dose.

THEC. A lingering death..

VOL. Then fall in love.

THEC. No; anything but that.

VOL. Like medicine, it may be unpleasant to the taste, but is very suitable as a tonic in certain cases. I said so, only yesterday, to that eccentric person, Count Julian of Toledo. Do you know him?

THEC. No.

VOL. A thousand pities! Quite a delightful young man, pleasantly different from most, who are measured by the yard, and cut from a common piece.

THEC. I admire his poetry, especially his 'Sappho,' and have heard much of him.

VOL. Do you know, Thecla, that, by some strange chance, the last shreds of my faith seem to hang round your glorious presence. I believe you capable of prodigies. Sometimes I almost think that, by a touch, you might restore the sick to health.

THEC. Then you believe in miracles?

VOL. Who shall say? Now here's a miracle I would propose to you. Count Julian——

THEC. That name again! How many times am I to hear of him this day?

VOL. This Galahad—this paragon prince of virtue—this loather of the sex—cause him to fall in love with you, and think of the added laurel to your crown.

THEC. A strange suggestion. To what end?

VOL. Merely as. a study in psychology. I design to write a comedy on love, and would sound to the bottom with a surgeon's probe. But I see you shrink. The difficulties are doubtless great.

THEC. I said not so.

VOL. Now, I will bet an aigrette of diamonds that you don't succeed.

THEC. And I accept the challenge. I am to recite to-night before the Court. *He* will be there. You say that he's romantic. He shall first see me in my character of muse. I will select the most impassioned verses from his 'Sappho,' and then——

VOL. Well planned. A bargain, mind. An enamelled snuff-box against a diamond aigrette.

> [*Page announces at door*, "The carriage of Her Highness the Princess of Novgorod."

THEC. My sister arrived from Russia after two years of absence. A surprise indeed!

VOL. (*sniffing*). I might have divined her advent from the sickly odour of virtue which suddenly pervades the room.

THEC. Voltaire, your ribaldry has been better placed.

VOL. Forgive me, but I cannot pardon her propriety. There is something aggressive in her manner of imposing virtue—as your Prussian king imposes peace—by force of arms.

THEC. Her name, which she values at so high a price, to be bandied thus! A bitter lesson for thee, proud Olivia.

VOL. Hark! The dragon rattles her scales, and juts forth her fierce tongue upon the stairs. Quick, Monsieur Laroque, we are *de trop.* I'm off. You will have half-a-hundred virtuous secrets to interchange.* Monsieur Laroque, I pray you, let us be discreet.

THEC. Thanks, thanks, Voltaire.

VOL. An excellent heart. Provided, of course, that hearts exist.　　　　　　　　　　　[*Exit* VOLTAIRE *and* LAROQUE.

Enter OLIVIA *in travelling dress, ushered by page, who exits.*

THEC. Olivia—sister!

OLIV. My Thecla.

THEC. At length we meet after two long years. How beautiful you have become. How bright your face. Then the Russian grandee has made you really happy?

OLIV. Is that so strange? The name of the Prince, my husband, is universally esteemed. Thank Heaven, he stands too high ever to be touched by calumny. Believe the experience of my maturer years; reverence freely tendered by the world is a great comfort.

THEC. Comfort! Have the happy then need of being sustained? You prate of esteem, of universal respect. Should there be no nearer tie?

OLIV. I am truly proud to bear the honoured name of Novgorod.

THEC. Icicles set in words. Do you love him—say—do you love your husband?

OLIV. I esteem him much.

THEC. Alas! no more.

OLIV. How could I do more? You know that my story is the same as yours; the story of most German ladies of our rank and fortune. The old sad story that is ever new. Married both to men who knew us not nor cared to know us, what more had we a right to ask? The love of which the poets sing is but the phantasm of a dream; a garland for prattling children to drape themselves withal. Our years have whispered wisdom to our hearts, have taught us that the world is the true god to worship—that before that brazen throne——

---

* It is necessary for Laroque to remain on during the foregoing scene, though mute. His presence will dispel the feeling of *tête-à-tête* too prominent through the act.

THEC. Sister, drop the mask. The world! What invisible Juggernaut is this? What right has the world to count the beatings of my pulse? I act according to the generous dictates of my heart, and can despise the verdict of the world!

OLIV. (*in an undertone*). And how I fear it, the terrible colossal phantom, with an overwhelming exaggerated fear! Call it weakness, nightmare, if you will. You are a widow, free, young, beautiful, and may, perhaps, despise, but I dare not follow in your steps. The human soul has need of love, and I feel sometimes as though I might yet love, but then between me and the object of my choice rises the cold ghost, and my blood flows back in frozen torrents on my heart.

THEC. Poor Olivia!

OLIV. As your breath of life is incense and applause, so do I live in calm respect. When I go abroad, I feel that my every glance is weighed, my every impulse sifted, and each whispered word makes me to blanch and tremble.

THEC. Beware, sister, of the path of self. It is as slippery as your fetish is insatiable. To-day you will toss your inclinations on its altar; to-morrow, if need be, the friendships of your youth. You will do it, for once started you may not recoil. You will cast all upon the blazing pile, at first with terror, then with indifference, at last with a wild joy bred by revenge for all that you have suffered from the seeming sacrifice. And when you shall stand in the solitude of death both God and altar shall alike melt away, leaving you alone amid your ruins; and the first voice raised to denounce and to upbraid you will be the voice of the idol fashioned by your hands.

OLIV. Peace, for pity's sake. You yourself have said it. Once on the incline, I must move onward, come what may.

THEC. You are right, and I am but a fool. Who am I that I should cloud your coming with boding words? Now you are mine, beloved Olivia, and for a long time. Is it not so?

OLIV. (*embarrassed*). No.

THEC. At least for several weeks.

OLIV. Indeed no. My husband's occupations——

THEC. (*bitterly*). Enough. Above all let us honour Truth. You fear what idle tongues clack forth of me. You are ashamed of me. Of me!

OLIV. Nay, sister——

THEC. Go your way, Olivia, on your solitary road. I pity you.

OLIV. Yes, pity me; for alas, indeed, I need it. I, cold and calculating as I seem to you, am most unhappy. My heart is warped through need of sympathy.

THEC. Where your heart speaks, listen to its words. A true heart is an unerring guide through the tangled maze of life.

OLIV. (*desperately*). Would you advise me thus? On your head be it then. You shall know what no living soul should guess. Calm as I seem, I love, Thecla, with all the wild torrent of passions long pent up; yet reason and judgment bid me suffocate my heart.

THEC. Wherefore?

OLIV. Because the man who loved me and offered me his love, though high in rank, was neglected and disgraced, and I dreaded the sarcastic comments of the world. Because he who is now a hero was then a princelet flying from his crown, prisoned by an angry sire. I deemed him doomed to an ignoble fate, and feared to accept his proffered hand. Had I but known that Frederick was to become the "Great!"

THEC. Hush! for Heaven's sake. Palace walls have ears, and Frederick's wrath once roused is not lightly to be lulled to rest. What selfish repining's this? Your path is more beset with danger than I thought. You must leave Berlin without so much as seeing the king. You came here purposely in hopes of meeting him. Is it so? For shame! I read it in your downcast looks.

OLIV. (*wildly*). I cannot—no! I cannot. I *will* see him once again if only to explain.

THEC. (*sternly*). Olivia, you forget yourself.

OLIV. (*spitefully*). So this is your boasted spurning of the world.

THEC. Sister, there is something higher than the world's esteem—respect for self. Come, your carriage is below. There is no time to lose, for he will presently be here. Nay, look not at me thus.

Enter SERVANT.

SERV. The Count of Toledo waits below.

THEC. 'Tis well.   [*Exit* SERVANT.
Come—you *shall* come—away.   [*Exeunt.*

Enter JULIAN, *with a letter in his hand.*

JUL. No one! Yet Laroque bade me lose no time, but prostrate myself at once before the intellectual queen. I thought to find a brilliant gathering. Are the adorers of the dread goddess vanished into air? So I am to meet the irresistible muse at last. The old tricks, I suppose; the well-worn attractions, with pompous mysterious noddings of the head, designed to mask the emptiness within. Heigho! How sick to death am I of clever women, for ever juggling their wares to drum and trumpet like cheap-jacks at a fair. There's something fantastic about this castle too. (*Sits.*) And this note, so daintily worded, so gracefully expressed. Now I'm prepared to swear that twenty just such notes have already been despatched this day. Happy they who can see truth in woman's guile. A book,—my Sappho! with pencilled thoughts upon the margin. What's this? "Sappho was right! In this base world the only end for those who really love is suicide. It is more difficult to know how to love than how to hate,—yet each one says he loves or hates. Fools! He to whom the mystery is locked yet feigns to have the key!" This earth-born goddess must be a singular woman.

> [*Behind curtain, in* O. *of flat, low and plaintive music, played on harps, something dreamy and sad,—say one of the "Songs without Words,"—the same music to recur at stated intervals. After a few bars* THECLA *is heard to declaim, through the music; behind the drapery, which is to be drawn aside by unseen hands as she speaks the last lines. It would be well to have the space behind the archway raised two steps, so as to give her the appearance of a statue when the curtain is drawn aside. Her pose and draperies should be very carefully studied.*

THECLA *declaims.*

"Poor's the mute heart with speech never blest;
Poor is the blossom uncrowned with perfume.
I glide through the world, my love unconfessed;
Like a lamp on an altar unknown, I consume.

JUL. Strange sentiments these for a successful woman!
None shall e'er guess the deep passion I cherish,
Love prisoned and numbed in a winter supreme,
(The lightnings of Heaven are born but to perish).
In the halls of the grave we shall slumber and dream.

JUL. Is it a heart that bursts its prison bars, or only an echo which murmurs mockingly?
Thrice hallowed the ashes that are heavenwards lifted;
Thrice blessèd the holocaust kindled above.
We spurn the dumb flower with scent never gifted,
As we grieve for the heart never opened to love."

> [*She pauses, and looks triumphantly at him before coming down the steps,—his back turned to her, sitting on an ottoman or sofa.*

JUL. Ah! She is here! How weirdly beautiful! Madam, you sent for me, and I came forthwith.

THEC. A thousand apologies, sir. Having to recite before the Court to-night, I am forced to snatch rehearsal hours when I may. I was repeating a few verses that answer to my thoughts.

C

Jul. And which I confess have waked in me chords long silent.

Thec. You have the reputation, Count, of being particularly severe upon us poor women, and yet I find you disposed to be indulgent; or are you, after all, a courtier like the rest?

Jul. Then, are those verses yours?

Thec. Strangely inharmonious as they are, I am forced to confess that they are mine.

Jul. Yours!

Thec. You seem vastly surprised! Your astonishment is scarcely galant!

Jul. Pardon me. I expected to find upon your young lips music of quite another character—more rhythmical, more beautiful, perhaps. The passion of these verses seems to rouse deep within my breast some vanished memory. (*Suddenly changing his manner.*) But really I am making myself quite ridiculous.

Thec. (*musingly*). Music of another character! Then much evil has been said to you of me.

Jul. No, Countess; not so. You were described to me as a splendid deity, the fascination of whose smile floods the dark recesses of men's souls with light. I was told that you are the muse of dreams—of golden, hazy, evanescent dreams; that around the sorceress floats an intoxicating atmosphere, the scent of which means death. You believe in love, they say; but your love is the laughing child of the arrow and the bow, who knows not tears. Your life is a life of feasting, over which oblivion is to cast an eternal veil.

Thec. For a portrait drawn at second-hand, it is not unlike. Let us commune of other things. My invitation to you appeared doubtless strange, but all I do is strange. Moreover, you are said to fly from us women as from a pestilence, which is not flattering; and we, haughty, revengeful dames, glory in bringing a foe as suppliant to our feet. Sir knight, you are betrayed! You came here as a guest, I detain you as a prisoner, fair booty of my sword and spear!

Jul. Never had prisoner so fair a gaoler. Yet beware; men were born to be ungrateful, and I may escape.

Thec. We amazons know well how to guard our prey.

Jul. Indeed! If I mistake not, your armoury holds none but flowery chains. Speedily woven, as lightly snapped in twain. How long, fair tyrant, is my durance to continue?

Thec. Till we learn to know each other better. Most men's souls are but shallow streams, to be sounded by a glance; but the soul of woman lies deeper than a well. Now come. Let us throw bantering aside, let us be straightforward and open one to the other. What do you think of me?

Jul. Truly and frankly?

THEC. Truly and most frankly. Yet stay. I can tell you beforehand what you think. You take me for a handsome, commonplace woman, without brains, a dreadfully good digestion, and an everlasting grin to show off the beauty of her teeth. If you believe all that the tattlers have to say of me, I will throw open the prison doors at once. Better, then, that we part almost ere we've met. (*A brief silence.*) Do you elect to go or stay?

JUL. I stay.

THEC. Then speak freely.

JUL. I believe you to be a woman who, but for circumstances, might have soared into an angel; but who, stricken down by doubt, has cast away her wings and fallen prone to earth. I believe you might have been some man's highest treasure, just as your bright laugh even now spreads happiness where'er you go. I take you for a woman who has something to forget—a fault perhaps—perhaps a disappointed hope; who firmly clasps her eyes with her own hands, nor dares to look around.

THEC. Thanks. Others see in me only a frivolous Sultana, a Fata Morgana with a heart of stone. Far from divining that I too was born to suffer, they would wring a smile from me even in the hour of my death. As the world could not give me what I sought, I accepted what it gave. I resolved at any price to reign, and, behold! I am but a poor play queen, spurning the fools who know not stage dross from gold.

JUL. And have you never loved?

THEC. No. Love as understood by those about us is but a mean welding of base subterfuge, of joyless joys, of fever without delirium. As I understand it, it may be a madness, but a sublime madness, which blots out the past, devours the present, annihilates the future. Who would have courage to love like this?

JUL. Are there, then, on earth, think you, no souls as generous as yours?

THEC. No doubt there are; but he who would find them must wade through such a slough of murky selfishness and egotism as well-nigh to sicken him into a renunciation of his race. I have renounced mine, have drowned it in the bowl of pleasure— have slain it outright.

JUL. Then I rightly solved your riddle?

THEC. Be not too sure of that. You and I are lightly discussing love, as we might discuss the war, the last mode, the last new tragedy. By-the-by, I have read your 'Sappho,' and like it much; but I hate Alçeon, your hero. With the mole-like blindness of his sex, he would make of woman either a slave or toy; would calculate to a nicety each heaving of her breast.

But what matter, after all? Would not her portion still be the balls and banquets, the rose wreaths and wax-lit chandeliers? What more, forsooth, should a well-brought-up damsel need?

JUL. Strange! In you there are two women. Which is the mask, and which the real face?

THEO. (*gaily*). Guess! I leave you now to ponder over this new riddle. Prisoner on parole, you have our gracious permission to wander in the park, where you may find a friend or two perhaps, empty-headed courtiers most of them, and one true man of genius, the great Voltaire. Good-bye. (*Archly.*) Meditate deeply over the gems of our discourse, or (*going off in a peal of laughter*) go and play skittles in the grounds.   [*Exit.*

JUL. She leaves me thus! What a fascination in her inspired look! Has she been merely toying with me, or has her haughty soul but hidden away this page from eyes too blind to read? But why, then, have revealed herself to me? A stranger, come to-day and gone to-morrow. Is this statue of marble or of clay?

LAROQUE *and* BARON ERFURT *without.*

LAR. I tell you, Baron, I know all about it. Who should be better informed than I?

JUL. Here come the popinjays who dance and flap their painted wings in the sunlight of her eyes. Why waste her charms on *them*—a daily, hourly, profanation.

[*Is going out, but stops.*

Enter LAROQUE *and* ERFURT *by the opposite door.*

ERF. Then, according to you, our star-crowned muse?——

LAR. One moment. Let us not misunderstand one another. I but chronicle a forgotten fact—a pearl dropped from history. "Once on a time, in a mighty city, rendered illustrious by heroes of the brain, there was a great lady and also an envoy from a foreign court." (*Julian draws himself up and listens near the door.*) "The envoy was an erratic youth, one of those overblown enthusiasts who always have a proverb pat upon their lips; who build of woman's virtue castles in the air, only to hurl stones of doubt at them, and erect ideal fortresses of love, glorious because they know naught of the reality."

ERF. 'Twere hard not to recognize the portrait.

LAR. "The ingenuous diplomat wandered over the surface of the earth, seeking his ideal like some hero of a fairy tale."

JUL. They speak of me!

LAR. "The great lady was passing fair. She had, moreover, registered a bet to conquer the invincible."

JUL. (*aside*). A bet!   [*Throws down his hat on chair.*

ERF. A bet!

LAR. I repeat, a bet—who should be so well informed as I?—"with a certain celebrated poet and philosopher, who on his side swore, under certain circumstances, to create on the subject a brand new comedy."

ERF. Voltaire!

LAR. Hush! In diplomatic circles names are guessed, but never spoken.

JUL. (*aside*). And so like all the rest she's perjured, false, and double-faced! Her sweet ways are base deceit and artifice.

ERF. And the result?

LAR. "The envoy knelt at the great lady's feet, communed alone with her, and then——"

ERF. Well, and then?

LAR. Alas! the rest is mystery!

JUL. (*advancing calmly*). I may possibly fill the gap in your romance.

LAR. }
ERF. } You here!

JUL. The envoy (as you will that such shall be his title) came —came and saw the fair one, fair as dreams of youth. From her lips fell words like balm upon long festering wounds, and for a brief moment he thought he had found the masterpiece of Heaven's handiwork—the spotless beaming one—the beautiful. And then the dream vanished as it came. The harp was there, but stilled, alas! Its keys were rusted, its chords were snapped. Finally, the bet is lost, and the new comedy will never see the light.

ERF. And the envoy?

JUL. (*taking up his hat, which he had thrown down when he advanced*). Resolved to go.

ERF. And he did well!

JUL. Who knows? Yes, he went away, blithe and merry-hearted; for had he not amused a great lady, two courtly butter-flies, and a world-renowned philosopher?—more than many a professed jester could ever hope to do.

LAR. (*slowly*). But I'm not so sure that I think——

JUL. And who in Heaven's name recks what you think? (*Coldly*). But ere he leaves the scene he will place this epitaph over the wan ashes of his trustfulness: "He found a false idol girt with lying worshippers; the first he pitied, the second he despised."

ERF. Have a care, young sir! The jest is broad, and, to say the least, ill-timed.

JUL. Is this a menace from the Lord of Erfurt? A duel! My Lord, for shame. Nay, put up your sword. Reserve its light-nings for a nobler purpose. We two are honest men, and honest hearts are now-a-days too rare for casual spitting on an idle point.

LAR. Well said! Let my winter cool your April blood! Best leave at once! and yet you cannot without first seeing the King. He will have come ere this.   He

> " Who by streaming locks
>   Holds victory enchained ;
>   Who, 'mongst primæval rocks,
>   Re-echoed by battle shocks,
>   Glory on glory gained."

Verses of mine, penned in his honour.   Ahem!   Neat.   The occasion is propitious.

JUL. Frederick *here*, say you?   How?

LAR. You must know that the King is fond of his incognito. His title of Count Hecksen, under which cognomen he seeks out his lieges, is a species of moral toga in which he wraps himself when——

ERF. (*laughing*). When it pleases him to play Haroun-al-Raschid.   Ah! apropos, great poet, your parable's deciphered, your impenetrable mystery unveiled, Ariadne is discovered.

LAR. Gentlemen! gentlemen!   *Pray* don't compromise me. A Court rhymster *never* mentions names.   My head, I do declare, feels quite loose upon my shoulders.

JUL. Of what Ariadne would you speak?

LAR. I pray you, Baron!

ERF. Of the beauteous nymph, sung by *his* immortal verse, whose lord has fled into a better sphere, and who has known how to console her widowhood with a wandering love.

JUL. (*smiling*). And so Bacchus is?——

ERF. (*nodding*). Ye—es.

JUL. And Ariadne?

ERF. Of course our heaven-inspired Countess.

JUL. She!   It is a lie!

ERF. Sir!

JUL. A lie, I say!—worse, a calumny black as hell, born of envy or revenge!

ERF. Know you well this fair one, whose colours you seem so anxious to fix upon your helm?

JUL. Enough if needful to sustain my words.

ERF. But I tell you he is here now, comes here almost daily under the shallow pretence of seeking her political advice.

JUL. Is this true, Monsieur Laroque?

LAR. Yes!   Though why he comes it is not for us to say— " He who by streaming locks holds victory enchained !"——

JUL. Lost, alas! perchance she may be, but a royal favourite never!   Which of you dare to say the word?

ERF. (*exasperated*). I! This fellow is unbearable!

JUL. (*menacingly*). I see, my Lord, that five yards of grass may yet be our lot!

ERF. When you please, sir! But here comes the King,—see how she hangs upon his arm!

Enter FREDERICK *and* THECLA, *arm in arm, passing round the front of the stage, from one door to the other, during their interview.*

FRED. And so you think war would be rash, against our cousin of France? Perhaps you're right, fair prophetess, as you generally are; but we will hear our other staunch adviser on the subject, our great Voltaire. I came to crave half an hour of your hospitality, to blot from my troubled brain awhile the tawdry glitter of statecraft; but Time, regardless of the wish of kings, moves on, and I must take my leave. Your castle, Countess, might be the stronghold of Armida herself.

THEC. Alas, sire, I fear the enchantress is wanting——

FRED. What sybil than yourself more fitted to give laws?

THEC. Oh, that I were indeed gifted with the mystic eye of dreams! To fathom——

FRED. What?

THEC. That which you keep so jealously concealed.

FRED. In policy?

THEC. No—in love. Confess, sire, that you came here to-day to see a lady?

FRED. Of course I did. Who loves me not, the fickle fair one.

THEC. Who loves you but too well.

FRED. (*looking at her*). Can it be? Why, then, her constant coldness?

ERF. (*to Julian*). Did I not tell you? Have you any doubt? See how they dally with each other's hands.

THEC. But tho' she loved you well, she forgot not her dignity or yours; and doubting her own strength, sought security in flight.

FRED. Who loves me well, you say?

THEC. Better even than I.

FRED. Of what lady would you speak!

THEC. I know all, sire. My sister was here but now, and has confessed.

FRED. Olivia of Novgorod at Berlin! No more. Stir not the leaves now shrivelled and decayed—crumbling rapidly to dust. Your sister, tho' once she plighted troth with me, submitted to union with another, because then I was a fugitive.

THEC. (*sighing*). Perchance 'tis better thus.

FRED. Tell her from me that she has naught to fear. This heart, that once was fire, shall now be steel to her. Nay! Tell her nothing. Enough of this. The sun is low, and I am waited for at Sans Souci. Gentlemen, good evening. Ah, Count Julian, poet and ambassador! You in a lady's castle? Fie! Where have you stowed your principles? To-morrow night the King holds Court, and will expect you all. Muse, warm me this statue—convert this Puritan—(*sees Julian glaring at him, then, with a laugh*)—Jealous of me, i' faith! The work then 's half begun.

THEC. I doubt it, sire.

FRED. Adieu, Countess, I kiss your hands. Tell Voltaire I expect my revenge for beating me at chess last night. Gentlemen, may I count upon your company?

[*Exit with* LAROQUE *and* ERFURT, *conducted to the door by* THECLA.

JUL. (*falling on a chair, and hiding his face in his hands*). Then it was all true!

THEC. (*approaching him*). How chilly! Stern as the tomb, as cold and silent. Well, Count, and what think you of our excellent Prussians?

JUL. Nothing!

THEC. A presumptuous reply.

JUL. I know them not.

THEC. Then study them.

JUL. Would they repay the trouble spent? I have travelled much; have found ever the same sickening routine of self-glorious vanity and falsehood over the whole surface of the earth. My life is spent in a weary search for that which never can be found.

THEC. The philosopher's stone?

JUL. (*after a contemptuous silence*). Why not? Your head-gear, Countess, is a miracle of art. Your dress is absolutely the *beau idéal* of good taste.

THEC. (*lightly*). Really?

JUL. It is true that in France that ribbon would be worn more highly poised——

THEC. Of a truth you are remarkably well versed in the latest mode! (*With increasing heat*). And is it fashionable just now in France to be for ever darkly groping for the unattainable? Is it the mode for the great ones there to be always pale and worn and rueful and resigned? Do the flower of its youth trick themselves in mystery, as in a tragic robe, welling with noble sadness, or burning with disdain? If such be the case, receive my heartfelt congratulations. You are yourself the very pink of fashion.

Jul. You see, Countess, that intercourse between us is impossible. It is not our fault; your genius takes too high a flight.

Thec. (*ironically*). Really! your perspicacity is something terrible.

Jul. I may be poor in tact, perhaps; but I strike always from the heart.

Thec. Shafts winged with pain! Our great Voltaire says——

Jul. Speak not to me of Monsieur de Voltaire.

Thec. Presently you will deny merit, even to him!

Jul. I admire and appreciate, without loving him.

Thec. Why?

Jul. Because we cannot love where we do not esteem.

Thec. Your aphorism is severe on M. de Voltaire.

Jul. Voltaire makes my blood curdle in my veins, with his arrogant contempt for the opinion of the world.

Thec. Ah! the murder's out! There's the terrible cant word launched at last. Public opinion! False echo of a thousand idle voices, which an infant's babble or an idiot's cry is sufficient to arouse, but which, once roused, naught shall still henceforth! Bow ye neck and knee before this awful majesty, whose robes are wrought from shadows, whose brow is wreathed in clouds! Pile up the altars till they seethe and flare with wrecked ambitions and with blighted hopes! Pour forth a libation of cherished memories!—and tell me then, what is this deity that you adore? An empty name—a substanceless chimera: worse still, a common courtesan, whose charms are purchased with a price. My poor Laroque, who is content to skim thro' life wearing the livery of a changeless smile—Baron von Erfurt, an adventurer whose head's as empty as his purse— these are the world! Pale parasites, who sit daily at my board, ready to curse or cringe, as suits their mood. The verdict of these, and such as they, is " public opinion." You worship and I defy it!

Jul. Words! Countess—dangerous words, which burn the lips that utter them. Listen to me. As wandering stars may meet by chance in the vast firmament on their heavenly pilgrimage, so have our lots, one sad, one joyous, crossed for a brief instant. To-morrow we shall go our ways,—you on the blossom-strewn path of pleasure and indulgence; I, solitary, ignored, derided maybe; seeking painfully but patiently for truth wherewith to kindle faith. One day my words may vaguely echo in your breast, as might Laroque's latest ode, or Erfurt's tales of love.

Thec. Count!

Jul. Remember or forget, I will tell you what I think. Lady, there are wars that must not be waged—battles that may not be fought. A woman's pride should never—*can* never resemble the pride of man. You say you have flung your glove full in the monster's face, have scorned and defied the world; but are you sure the potent hand will never be raised to strike? And even granted that it could be so, that all thro' life you might be allowed to spurn and gag the mysterious power, none the less will your purity have lost its lustre, none the less will your robe of whiteness have become dabbled and smirched with mire. The terrible unseen one will have wrapped you in his hundred arms, will have sullied your brow with the touch of his thousand lips, have howled your name aloud with his myriad tongues; and a woman's name must ever be breathed with bated breath, lest the snow be defiled with which it should be crowned.

THEC. (*ironically*). Why, you are an improvisatore as well as a poet, fit almost to join our philosophical court. It is a pity such fine words should be lost on sterile ground.

JUL. (*impetuously*). Woman! are you an angel or a fiend?

THEC. (*lightly*). Probably neither one nor other, or rather, perhaps, both. "More angelic than the angels," as Laroque tearfully remarked last night, in an access of admiration due to my French cook. For am I not a *woman?* But the shock of battle too long sustained is wearing to the brain, and, as a woman, I have a wholesome dread of wrinkles. Remember you are the victim of my sword and spear. We have material for at least a week's tournament.

JUL. I decline the honour of the contest.

THEC. (*clapping her hands*). Bravo! An unconditional surrender! by all known laws of warfare. Are we Prussians, then, to gather laurels upon every field?

JUL. Where there is no conflict there can be no defeat.

THEC. Oh! How like poor man's petty vanity! And why, pray, do you decline to fence with me?

JUL. Because I am about to take my leave.

THEC. Depart from the castle?

JUL. And from Prussia.

THEC. So suddenly? I won't believe it.

JUL. I go, I say.

THEC. When?

JUL. To-morrow.

THEC. And when did you make this grand resolve?

JUL. Now.

THEC. Be it as you will. But your fervid eloquence has degenerated with alarming promptness into monosyllables. Adieu, then. But how about your embassy?

JUL. It will be in safe hands.

THEC. A diplomatic answer truly! The king was right when he said——

JUL. (*impatiently*). Countess, farewell.

THEC. Do we then meet no more?

JUL. No.

THEC. (*smiling*). Really?

JUL. What purpose would another meeting serve?

THEC. Not even courteous, on my word! Your solemn retreat with bag and baggage looks dreadfully like flight. Beware, lest I pursue and it become a rout! I believe that you are afraid.

JUL. Of whom?

THEC. Either of me or of yourself.

JUL. Lady; I have watched children crush the butterfly that lighted on the window-pane for very wantonness. I have marked others idly shattering in play the flower which bloomed upon their path.

THEC. Go on, sir.

JUL. And then, I have turned from my way to avoid saying, "The work of your hands is contemptible and base."

[*Bows coldly and exit.*

THEC. (*after a pause of bewilderment*). He scorns me. He! Neither he nor any one. He may learn to hate, but shall never dare to scorn. Disdain and insolence from *him!* After all, what matters it? Are there not hundreds here who prize my lightest favour? But 'twixt them and he, oh! what a gulf is there! What is this fiery breath which burns my cheek? Offended vanity!—no more. If he were indeed never to return. (*Takes a hand-glass from the table and surveys herself.*) But he will—he will return!

VOLTAIRE (*putting in his head through* C. *curtains*). Alone?

THEC. Alone!

VOL. Has he long been gone?

THEC. He went but now.

VOL. And he loves you, of course, already?

THEC. (*slowly and doubtfully*). Aye. He loves me!

VOL. Wretched man.

THEC. (*wildly*). Nay, say rather, most wretched woman!

[*Falls on a seat and buries her face on the table.*

VOL. Stand matters thus? (*Standing over her.*) Then wretched woman, truly! I positively almost believe in the most absurd of human passions—Love! But Voltaire *may* not believe. The world would laugh too much! [*Curtain.*

Tableau II. *Exterior of Palace of Sans Souci, near Berlin.*
Scene divided. On P. side, illuminated doorway at back,
leading into ball-room, with flight of five or six steps leading up
to it. Trees with Chinese lanterns, garden chairs, &c. This
set to occupy two-thirds of the stage. On O.P. side, a pavilion,
occupying about from first to third grooves, with door leading
to park, and secret door at back masked by a picture. Table
with candles and a silver dish ; seats. The distinctions of
colour should be strongly marked. Thus, the shrubbery and
adjuncts should be cool *and* green, *and the interior of pavilion*
red *and* warm. *Outside the pavilion door, a small flat of cut-*
out scenery at R. *angles with pavilion, masking upper entrance*
on O.P. *side. The small flat to represent bushes, with a statue*
of Cupid blindfold. Under the statue, practicable marble seat.
Dance music at intervals behind scenes.

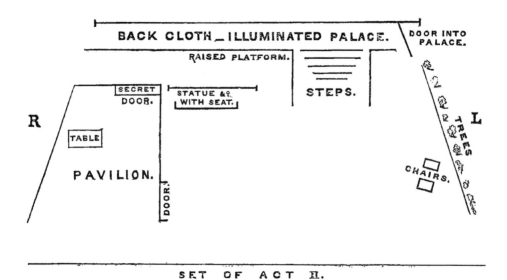

Enter Laroque, *reading from a paper.*

" When glorious Mars bestrode his mighty horse,
    And rushed victorious along his starry course,
    Ne'er was his path bestrewn with wreaths so thick
    As those that strew the path of Frederick ! "

There. That's a beautiful ending to a first-rate ode. Now no
one would guess how difficult it is to turn an heroic rhyme to

Frederick, and yet the man's deeds speak for themselves. There's sick, and quick, and lick,—but they can *not* somehow be made to sound heroic. If I could only find the king, and recite these verses to him, he'd name me Court poet at once; but he's left the ball this hour, and no one knows where he's gone. If the northern Muse were gone too, it might not be so surprising; but there she is in the ball-room, like some triumphant Pallas, holding a brilliant court of her own. The cynosure of all eyes, admired of all admirers; more especially since it is known that the king ——Well, it's natural in her, for is not woman frail? (*Sits under statue.*) And yet the situation's complicated. There's this Count Julian, the Puritan, to whose society she seems so unaccountably attached. But who shall blame her? She has her position to make, like all of us, and is making it. Every satellite revolves around this star, while the spotless Princess Olivia sits alone. Ah, me! they may say what they like, but propriety is no longer the fashion. Not but what our poor Countess is quite proper—oh, quite proper!—but—what's this? A handkerchief —lost in the park—near the king's private pavilion. Very suspicious indeed. Just now, in the ante-room, I found on the floor, by strange coincidence, this note :—"Frederick : After the third dance, I shall expect you in the pavilion near the statue. Come." Brief, unsigned, but to the point; and cautious, too. Mr. Cupid, you are certainly the presiding deity here. The whole place is seething with love-tokens.

Enter, down steps, ERFURT *and* VOLTAIRE.

ERF. So you never condescend to dance, M. de Voltaire?

VOL. No, sir, I leave that to monkeys and popinjays.

ERF. And yet, if I mistake not, even now, in yonder room, there are celebrated men engaged in the innocent enjoyment of a quadrille. Invincible generals, statesmen of unknown depth.

VOL. Earnestly occupied in playing the fool.

ERF. But, according to the teaching of your own immortal works, the age of Reason will soon dawn on us, and then how happy shall we be! (*Very glibly, without full stops.*) Equality in instruction, equality of institutions, equality in wealth! All men are brothers; why not, then, inaugurate a universal language? The organic perfectability of the vegetable world being undisputed, why should Nature be less powerful in the nobler existence of thinking man? The destruction of the two most active causes of decay, luxurious wealth and abject penury, will certainly prolong the general term of life. Medicine shall be honoured in the place of war, which is the art of murder. The noblest study of the acutest minds shall be devoted to the arrest of the causes of disease; and, as the lower animal bequeaths its

vigour to its offspring, so man shall transmit his improved
organization to his sons——

VOL. (*holding his ears*). Stop! stop! in mercy! He winds
off the anxious study of long years like a skein upon a reel.
Have I preached and thought only to be caricatured by parrots,
who glibly mouth that they cannot comprehend? Alas! alas!
what credit to be wise in the midst of a world of fools!

LAR. (*behind*). Philosophy is the fashion just now in the
intellectual court to which we have the honour to belong.

VOL. Yes; young dandies learn to put it on as they don their
coats, or sprinkle powder in their hair.

ERF. What would you have, M. de Voltaire? We follow
only in your steps humbly, at a respectful distance. You are
the head of a new school. My hairdresser said to me, this
morning,—"Though but a poor fellow, Baron, I believe as little
as the finest gentleman." And the man was honest.

VOL. Words, words, young sir.

ERF. Do you not, then, believe in honesty?

VOL. When it suits my purpose, I believe the moon to be made
of cheese. But what do you here in solitude, M. Laroque,

> "'Mid leafy groves, beneath the azure vault,
> Sparkling with myriad gems"?

Are you, too, weary of railing at the world, or are you hatching
a new sonnet, as ostriches sit upon their eggs, alone in the wide
desert? It's a melancholy profession, that doesn't pay. Depend
on it, none should turn poet who are capable of hewing wood or
drawing water—more healthy and more lucrative.

LAR. (*rising and coming forward*). No. I was meditating on
history.

VOL. Another dreary occupation—the study of our fellow
man!

ERF. Sacred, or profane?

LAR. On contemporary history. See. [*Shows handkerchief.*

VOL. A strange book! the page of finest cambric.

LAR. Adorned with an embroidered crest.

ERF. A crest! I should recognize it, but cannot recall to
mind—— I have certainly seen it before, but where?

LAR. This kerchief was lost here, close to the pavilion where
Frederick is said to meditate and love.

ERF. They say his love's compounded of politics and sawdust,
dull pastime for young ladies surfeited with dolls.

LAR. At any rate, it's very suspicious; there's no denying
that.

ERF. Stay, I have it. A tiger rampant, supporting a sword.
The crest of the noble family of Herfland.

LAR. The family of the Lady Olivia!

ERF. And of the Lady Thecla.

VOL. (*aside*). Verily the human mind loves a sharp bit of scandal, as donkeys thistles!

LAR. Which can it be?

ERF. Is there room for doubt? If the good name of the Princess Olivia is not in itself enough, enter yonder, where the crowd that salutes the rising sun will show clearly which it is.

LAR. If it were indeed she!

ERF. You've come upon a precious talisman, for by the help of this artless scrap of white fabric we might strike upon the trace of a whole romance.

LAR. One moment, Baron, one moment. That talisman has been taken from me who found it, to whom it appertains by right, and I solemnly reclaim it. Give it me.

VOL. So do vultures rend their plumes over a feast of garbage. I'm prepared to swear in favour of the virtuous sister, but it's no affair of mine.

ERF. (*laughing*). What—ambitious, M. Laroque? Would you change this dainty token 'gainst a place?

LAR. Why not? Many a fortune has risen upon a more slender basis.

ERF. Oh! most unselfish poet, whose eyes can turn from Parnassus down to common earth! Take it, it's yours. And may it bring you happiness. Here comes Prince Novgorod, mirror of ancient aristocracy.

VOL. Then I'll *decamp*. His wife's odour of sanctity hangs round him too. Pah!   [*Exit* R.U.E.

NOVGOROD *comes down steps.*

LAR. The very occasion—his influence! You must introduce me.

NOV. Well met, Baron. I am forced to come out and breathe the air, so disgusted am I and overwhelmed by all I see and hear.

ERF. Indeed, Prince! This is bad news. Does the Prussian Court not please you?

NOV. I verily know not on what world I stand. Have I been sleeping for a thousand years? After a lengthened sojourn in the Courts of Europe, I, two years since, as it seems to me, retired with my bride to my estates upon the Volga. And now that I take up once more my old career, what do I find? Surely my eyes and ears deceive me. A king, who receives *me*, ambassador—*me*, Prince of Novgorod, in boots and spurs. A Court where one risks at every turn to find oneself elbowed familiarly by some low writing fellow with probably no shirt beneath his coat, whose snuff is fuller's-earth, and who at one time would have been honoured by admittance to the kitchen.   I find every sacred law of etiquette held up to ridicule, every antique privilege forgot.   While to crown all, behold a French Envoy on a secret mission, who thereby is placed on the same rank with *me*, and who has absolutely *no ancestors*, not the smallest twig of a family tree !   A sort of scribbler, who gabbles an incomprehensible jargon, while his fingers are thick begrimed with ink.

ERF. But who happens to be called Voltaire.

NOV. A name quite unknown, as I 've been informed.

ERF. Pardon me, Prince, too well known, some say ; though here we acknowledge in him a master born to transform the world.

NOV. What does it all mean ?   The earth slides from beneath my feet, and my head goes round.   Is he an ambassador who amuses himself by playing the philosopher ?

VOL. (*who is crossing and going up steps on way to ball-room, but who stopped on hearing his name*). No, your Highness ; only a philosopher who spends his spare time in playing the ambassador.   Your humble servant.   [*Exit into Palace.*

NOV. What means that mocking smile of his ?   I almost believe he dares to laugh at *me !*

LAR. Present me to the Prince.   I have important things to say to him.

ERF. Allow me, Prince.   Count Adam de Laroque-Tournai.

NOV. A very ancient French family, though poor.   It pleases me to touch your hand.

LAR. Prince, you are too good.

ERF. A distinguished literary character.

NOV. What, he too !   In my young days, a man of gentle birth would rather die of starvation than join a company of merry-andrews.   But times are sadly changed.

ERF. You have something urgent, you say, for His Highness's ear ?   Then I will go and bask in the new sun's rays awhile. My lord, I take my leave.   [*Exit up steps.*

NOV. You have something you would communicate to me, sir ?

LAR. I have desired the honour of knowing your highness, because I flatter myself I may, perhaps, be of some poor use to you.   Moreover, the veneration that I have for the name of Novgorod, whose origin looms dimly through the night of time——

NOV. Yes, yes ; I am aware of my illustrious descent.   Proceed.

LAR. Prince.   Are you certain we 're not overheard ?   I have a painful fact to reveal to you, which, once divulged to vulgar ears, might compromise your noble name in the face of Europe, whose eyes are ever fixed with reverence on you. In these degenerate days, when the sad duty falls to us of keeping ward over our privileges assailed, we must be united, and help each other in order to be strong.

Nov. The speech of a true gentleman.

LAR. I hope so. (*Mysteriously.*) Ahem! Restore this kerchief to whom it belongs. Lost here, by the King's door. Look at the crest.

Nov. (*stamping his foot*). Thecla! Will you always shower shame upon us! What does not your folly cost me! Poor Olivia! how sweetly different art thou from thy madcap sister! But, excuse me, sir. This secret affects the honour of a noble house.

LAR. A secret known to none, and buried.

Nov. Count of Laroque Tournai, we bestow on you our friendship.

LAR. Thanks, prince. You honour me too highly. But, see; here the lady comes.

Nov. Ah! the sooner the better.

(*Enter* THECLA *and* JULIAN *down steps.*)

THEC. Let us close our argument in the soft summer air, that the breeze may scatter our foolish words. I assure you we shall both be gainers.

JUL. No, Countess; yours I bind together in a posy, to prison in the casket of my heart, that their sweetness may permeate my life.

THEC. All these are terribly like a courtier's compliments, and I hear so many each weary day.

Nov. (*advancing*). Countess von Thürenau.

THEC. My dear brother-in-law, as I live! Are you here in dutiful attendance on my sister? What a model husband, and how doubly blessed a wife! Welcome to the frivolities of Sans Souci. Has the amiable atmosphere of corruption, wafted to us from beyond the Rhine, succeeded yet in melting the icebound tracts of your frowning Neva? Do tell me, is every one in Russia as coldly virtuous as you? How dull it must be there! Must it not, Count Julian of the sunny South?

Nov. Countess—dally not thus idly with serious things. It becomes neither your youth nor the wisdom you choose to assume. I have a word to say to you in private.

THEC. In private! Heaven protect me, what an awful declaration! I protest; I shiver from top to toe! Gentlemen, will you excuse me? It shall not be for long. (*Julian and Laroque retire.*) Well, Prince, I listen.

E

Nov. Your family springs from an illustrious root, though much less old than mine.

Theo. (*drily*). Ahem! Might we not in mercy begin nearer home than Charlemagne? Trespass not on my patience! Would you speak of virtue or of duty? Then need you delve no deeper than my dead father's name—a revered one which is a never-failing charm. Beware how you use it lightly!

Nov. Then in his name will I speak now. Your folly, without limit, is a disgrace to your sister and to me. You have a high position, a princely fortune, and an ancient title to sustain intact before the world. How do you fulfil your sacred duty?

Theo. (*first angry, but turns it off with a laugh*). Prince! Pshaw! Too stupendous an exordium for me not to take fright at what's to come. Fie! A sermon in the midst of a ball! A death's-head disguised in flowers! And you an ancient diplomate!

Nov. You have misused your natural advantages—have renounced every privilege of your rank. You live like a gypsy 'mid a herd of mountebanks. Your strange relations with the King, though doubtless pure and above reproach——

Theo. Enough! you trespass on my good-nature. Have you aught else to say?

Nov. Yes, (*mysterious*) I have to return this kerchief, lost by *you there!* It was a grave imprudence, only removed from crime in that no one saw it. Thank your guardian angel that you're safe.

Theo. This kerchief! Ah! (*With emphasis.*) Yes, a grave imprudence truly, but one which may be repaired, and *shall,* I promise you! Thanks.

Nov. Good-night, Countess! Reflect upon my words.

[*Exit up steps.*

Lar. (*coming down on her other side*). That kerchief was found by one of your most devoted slaves, who chanced upon this letter also. [*She reads, and hides it in her bosom.*

Theo. I understand. Your silence, wily courtier, must be bought. You seek the nomination of which we spoke a few days since. It shall be yours! You have my word!

Lar. Fair muse, the worship of a life!——

Theo. A truce to protestations! Go!

Lar. Behold me poet-laureate! The longed-for wreath of bay upon my brow! I'll seek His Majesty at once! "When glorious Mars bestrode his mighty horse!" [*Exit declaiming.*

Julian comes down.

Theo. (*pensive*). Oh, Olivia! Olivia, sister! After your solemn promise!

JUL. Dearest muse, you seem to have become, in very truth, a marble statue. So pale, so serious. Nay, now the stone returns to life! You are agitated!

THEC. I! A passing cloud, such as at times o'ershadows all our lives. Listen to me, Julian, for I am in a serious mood. It is time to throw half confessions to the winds. You say you love me. You *do* love me! I feel—I know it! My soul whispers the sweet words to me! I hear it in your silence rather than your speech. (*Tenderly laying her head on his breast.*) And I love thee, my Julian! Wherefore should I hide it? I love thee.

JUL. Yes, Thecla. Strange being! In spite of myself, I love! Reason struggled hard against my passion, but is conquered, and has given up the fight. I have fought and wrestled with myself in vain. My fate is in your hands, enchantress, to be woven as you list for weal or woe.

THEC. Not so, Julian; our fates are in each other's hands. Architects of our own future, it remains for us to build a life of joy or sorrow for ourselves. Oh! may we not cast our happiness away. Let us act with prudence, for with ardent souls like ours there can be no middle course. It must be heaven or hell! Say, Julian, have you the courage to raise your head and proclaim aloud, This one reputed lost is the lady of my choice? Are you strong enough never to let the noisome breath of doubt for a moment stain the mirror of your faith?

JUL. My Thecla——

THEC. (*putting her hand on his lips*). No, not yet. 'Twere rash.

JUL. I will never doubt thee.

THEC. Alas! Vows have oft been broken!

JUL. Am I then of so little faith? (*smiling*). Give me that rose that it may nestle near my heart, and whisper thy name to me in dreams——

THEC. Not now. If you prove true I will give it in token that I am yours for ever. And now, take time rather than be forsworn. Return to the ball, and listen to the idle things they may say there of me. Then reflect deeply ere you finally decide. To-night we will meet no more. To-morrow, if you come not to the castle——

JUL. I shall have quitted Prussia.

THEC. You have understood me. (*Music within.*) The third dance! Go, Count. Leave me. Adieu.

JUL. Say rather, *au revoir.*

THEC. (*passionately*). Perhaps. [*Exit* JULIAN *up steps.* If I should but lean upon a broken reed! But he is not as other men. Yet at the thought my heart stands still!

[*Dance music, piano, behind scenes.*

Enter VOLTAIRE *down steps, who bows to* JULIAN *as he passes.*

VOL. Well, my brilliant child, and have I won the bet?

THEO. (*passionately*). Voltaire, what have you done? I love that man!

VOL. Then you shall lend your valuable experience and help to write the comedy.

THEO. Best wait to see the end. Hush! Some one comes!

VOL. A mysterious lady, veiled! Oh, shade of virtue, I thought as much!

THEC. Come, Voltaire—come away with me.

                     [*They retire in shadow of statue.*

Enter OLIVIA, *veiled, by first entrance* L.

OLIV. The alley is deserted, though I thought I heard voices. I can no longer bear this withering suspense, but *will* see and speak with him, come what may. I spied the key on entering, and took it from the lock. (*Turning in terror.*) Ah! No one— only the wind among the leaves. Now is my time.

         [*Enters pavilion, and closes door rapidly; as she does so,*
             ERFURT *appears at top of steps, makes a gesture of*
             surprise, and departs.

VOL. Oh, Goddess of Propriety! I sniff the virtuous presence of the Princess Olivia!

THEO. Alas, Voltaire! I pray you, silence. Come with me.

                         [*Exeunt* R.U.E.

OLIV. (*sinks on a seat in pavilion*). Heaven! Is it just that I should suffer thus? Spite of myself, a mysterious force drags me on till I totter over a precipice. A mystic chain of iron binds me hand and foot, and a will other than my own forces my presence here. I will see his face once more, will tell him how I really loved him, that I am not the vile creature that he thinks, and then will return my weary way, consoled. Oh, Frederick, Frederick! do I not love thee still?

                     [*Buries her face in her hands.*

Enter, down steps, ERFURT *and* LAROQUE.

ERF. Yes, yes. I tell you the pavilion's inhabited. Now to un-nest this timid dove. With my own eyes I saw her go in.

LAR. Who?

ERF. A lady, unless it can be an angel, though if it be she must be a slightly fallen one. No, an angel having wings would have preferred the chimney. Very decidedly a mortal woman.

OLIV. How late he is. The precious moments fly. What if he were not to come? What if my absence from the ball were to be remarked? But, no. All think me closeted with the Queen Mother.

ERF. The Princess Olivia! My good friend, you're dazed. The idea's preposterous. If I saw it with my eyes I'd not believe it. 'Tis against the preaching of our new philosophy.

LAR. But I tell you I met and bowed to her sister in the corridor not two minutes since.

OLIV. (*in the pavilion, walking up and down feverishly*). He comes not! he comes not! If he could measure my anguish, if he could know with what anxiety I wait, he would be more pitiful.

LAR. Are you certain this is the only door?

ERF. Most certain.

LAR. And she must pass this portal?

ERF. Undoubtedly, and we shall see her.

LAR. Supposing she were masked?

ERF. As a captain of His Majesty's body-guard, I have a right to know who wanders furtively at night within the royal precincts.

LAR. But the King——

ERF. Is engaged elsewhere. Besides, who knows better than he that a good soldier blindly obeys his orders?

Enter VOLTAIRE, R.U.E.

VOL. Gentlemen, gentlemen! In a pensive frame to-night, sighing at the yellow moon? Are you in love, or do you plot treason against our good Frederick? I should have thought the magnums of claret in the supper-room much more in your line.

ERF. Ah, great master! Your advent is well timed. We are ready to prove to you——

VOL. That man is the least rational of all the animals? I learnt that ere you were born. Don't waste your time teaching me old saws. The claret will repay you better.

LAR. (*to* ERFURT). Let us withdraw a little and watch, for fear of frightening our bird. Are you with us, M. de Voltaire? [*Music behind ceases.*

VOL. Thank you, no. When a performance is more than usually ridiculous, I prefer a warm seat among the audience to a cold caught among the actors.

LAR. Let us go, then. [*Exeunt, third grooves,* L.

VOL. (*taking snuff*). Thecla prays me to lure these men away. Shall I, for her sake, act contrary to well-worn principles, and lend a helping hand? No. It's a bad precedent. Let the imbroglio unravel itself, and sham virtue pilot its vessel to a haven if it can. [*Exit up steps.*

OLIV. (*turning to door*). I thought I heard a key grinding in a lock. It is not here. (*Turns and sees* FREDERICK, *who comes through the picture.*) Frederick!

FRED. (*coldly*). Yes, princess, 'tis I, in answer to your summons. I fear I've made you wait, not willingly, I beg you to believe; but the King has a thousand cares: an important review to organize for to-morrow, a council to be held with generals, envoys from abroad to hear and answer. Pardon me, princess, technical details can scarcely interest you. You asked for a secret interview. You have it. Speak.

OLIV. His frozen speech chills my words upon my lips.

[*Sinks on her knees.*

FRED. Well. You seem to have that to speak which finds difficulty in utterance. Is it not singular? Were a stranger to see us thus—you flushed, confused, with lowered eyes; I, calm and smiling—he might be led to think that he saw a fair criminal on bended knee before a benign judge, did he not know, which he could not fail to learn, that the Princess of Novgorod was never criminal, and that Frederick the Second never forgives.

OLIV. Sire, cease this leaden comedy.

FRED. Princess! When Frederick deigns to appear in comedy, it is on the wide stage which is called the world. Speak on, we wait your pleasure.

OLIV. The Empress of Russia sent my husband here as ambassador; I could not do less than follow him.

FRED. Why excuse yourself? We are duly thankful to Elizabeth; for a beautiful ambassadress is more to our taste than a wooden ambassador with a whalebone spine. Unless our memory fail us, you were here, unmarried, some few years back. Then can you tell our cousin of Russia that the ill-used Hereditary Prince has vanished beneath the king's diadem, and that Frederick the Second is altogether another man.

OLIV. Has Frederick, then, forgotten all?

FRED. Who studies and dissects the passions, learns to laugh at them.

OLIV. Then it will be easier for me to speak; for I am impelled to speak, sire, of a hapless lady, who loved the Crown Prince with a deep and fervent love.

FRED. Indeed! And what, in Heaven's name, would this lady of the King?

OLIV. She fears lest the King should have been deceived concerning her; lest he should see her actions through a discoloured light. There were strong motives for her line of conduct, of which the King may yet be ignorant. She would implore the King to bury reverently his memory of her, and then (*sobbing*) with tender hand to strew her grave with the immortal blossoms of regret.

FRED. She would have the King forget her? Re-assure the lady for me. Tell her the King not only forgets, but even adds the most complete indifference, although that lady's selfishness darkened and blighted his youth. Have you no more to add?

OLIV. (*in a suffocated voice*). No more.

[*She rises from her knees.*

FRED. Then our interview is at an end. You may go.

[*She totters to the door.*

By-the-bye, in the grove, without, a few hair-brained young men, distraught with idleness, are waiting, who have vowed to see the face of the lady who entered here. 'Tis but a silly jest, but, of course, the reputation of the Princess Olivia will silence all whisperings.

OLIV. Oh, sire, this is horrible! Betrayed by you! But there is another door.

[*Rushes to the picture.* FREDERICK *interposes.*

FRED. (*coldly*). That entrance is reserved for the persons who are dear to His Majesty. You, princess, are not one of those.

OLIV. Sire, sire! As you are great, have mercy on me, forget the past. I am but a feeble woman, and your revenge would not hunt down so weak a quarry? Poor in all that makes life beautiful, I've naught to live for but the world's respect, which is as air and light to me. To please the insatiate world, I have torn, one by one, the fibres of my heart, till it has grown a withered thing. Mercy! mercy, sire!

FRED. When our past, of which you spoke just now, lies mouldering in a common heap of ashes, then will the King of Prussia reply to the Princess of Novgorod.

[*He takes letters from a casket, burns one by one, leaving ashes in a silver dish.*

OLIV. Alas, alas! *My* letters! All is indeed over now.

[*Sinks on chair, and buries her face in hands.*

Enter VOLTAIRE, *down steps in park, with a letter.*

VOL. Here, in due form, is my recall to France. The King has, it seems, forgiven Mahomet, and languishes for my return; or is it that he has a snug little apartment in the Bastile awaiting me? I shall, indeed, be glad to go, as this spectacle is really too insipid. With all their trumpet-blowing and banging of drums, everything is hollow and below contempt. Their virtue is veneer, their philosophy an echo. They are true to themselves only in all-pervading greed and malice. Our age of reason must commence elsewhere. Ah, Count Julian.

(Enter JULIAN, R.U.E.)

JUL. It must be here; near the statue, by the door of the pavilion. 'Tis well. Here I am to meet this Baron Erfurt, whose pedantic ways are so insufferable.

VOL. I smell a rat. They 've sent him here to find—— Oh, how base is man! I 've half a mind to spoil this silly trick. The discomfiture of the mischief-makers will repay me for being weak enough to meddle in the troubles of fellow-fools. *(Advancing)*. Count Julian!

JUL. *(turning)*. Voltaire!

VOL. Baron Erfurt gave you rendezvous here for the generous purpose of surprising a lady, supposed to be shut up in the pavilion. Is it not so?

JUL. *(angrily)*. What lady?

VOL. The action would be mean enough were she a stranger, would it not? But supposing her to be one dear to you, it would be——

JUL. More infamous still.

VOL. I quite agree with you. Then, will you stay here as mere tool and accomplice of empty-headed Erfurt's little plots?

JUL. *(hesitating)*. I would not so disgrace myself.

VOL. Ah, that was what I wished to know. Not being a woman, I thought there might be some hope of your combating your curiosity.

JUL. You shall see. I await the Baron, to fling my glove in his face.

VOL. Well said.

FRED. All is over now.

OLIV. Are you inexorable, Frederick?

FRED. No. I have compassion on you. I merely wished you to tremble for that which you hold dearest on earth—your lying reputation, and showed you how easily it could be overthrown. Now I say to you, This worldly respect by which you breathe and live; behold, I give it you as alms! Return to the homage and admiration of the world. Return unspotted to pursue your arid way. The past exists no more. Behind that picture you will find a secret stair, leading, by an obscure corridor, to my mother's ante-chamber. Go.

OLIV. Oh, Frederick! *(He bows coldly. She recedes again.)*
Sire!   . [*She is going.* FREDERICK *moves the picture.* THECLA
           in a black cloak, with mask in hand, stands pale in
           the opening.
Thou!

FRED. You here, Thecla? How?

THEC. I tracked your steps. Pardon me, sire, but my sister was to be saved.

OLIV. Saved! What do you mean?

THEC. A lady was seen to enter here. This handkerchief, embroidered with the crest of both of us, was picked up near the door. They wait without to see one of us two pass.

OLIV. Oh, Heaven!

THEC. Therefore one of us two must go out by that door, or both are lost.

OLIV. Oh, I have not strength. I should droop and die.

THEC. No, you will not die; for I, who am here, can and will save you. Take this mask and domino. At the postern-gate a carriage waits, without livery or arms. Yours I sent home long since. You are supposed to have returned to your palace. Lose not a moment. Your husband has but now left the ball, and may suspect if you delay. Go. Fly!

OLIV. But you, sister.

THEC. (*with a bitter smile*). I! what have I to lose or gain? I despise the world.

OLIV. No, no; I could not suffer this. The fault is mine; be mine the punishment.

> [*Goes towards door; at this moment,* LAROQUE, ERFURT, *and a few guests come, laughing, down the steps. She hears them, recoils, kisses her sister's hands, and saying wildly,* "Forgive me, sister, but I dare not face them," *dashes through the panel, which closes after her.*

FRED. (*who has watched with crossed arms*). I knew it. A nature of stone, selfish to the core.

THEC. (*passes her hands over her brow*). Poor sister! rather pity her, for she deceives herself.

JUL. (*advancing to* ERFURT). Baron Erfurt; before leaving the palace, it is my duty to tell you that a wilful soiler of reputations is among the most dastardly of men. You will know where to find me.

ERF. At your service, sir.

JUL. Adieu and thanks, M. de Voltaire.

VOL. Begone; nor look behind. Remember Lot's wife.

THEC. (*with an effort*). Now, sire, I am ready. Give me your hand, and open yonder door. Let us go.

FRED. You are too noble for me to do aught but bow before your will. Raise your brow, Countess, that its light may shine on them.

LAR. Hush! The door moves. Be ready, Baron Erfurt.

ERF. In the King's name, who goes there?

> [JULIAN, *who stands at top of steps, with back to audience, turns his head.*

FRED. The King of Prussia and the Countess von Thürenau. Remove your hat, sir, and precede us to the ball-room.

[*Knocks off* ERFURT'S *hat.*

LAR., ERF., and GUESTS. The King !

FRED. Why do you smile, Count of Laroque-Tournai ? Is it some new epigram—another effusion on Bacchus and Ariadne ? Your French birth should lead you to remember that prison cells are very cooling to over-heated brains.

LAR. (*stammering*). I, sire, smile ? Never was more serious in all my life.

VOL. I declare, if I were not Voltaire, I would like to be Frederick the Second.

> [*They move towards steps.   Thecla is on the King's left arm ; therefore, on turning up steps, she comes face to face with Julian, who is* C. *of stage at top of steps.*

THEC. (*starting*). He here. The only one in all the world whom I would have far from hence ! Oh, Fate, thou art remorseless ! (*Drops King's arm.*) I pray you, sire, leave me. I am ill. I suffocate for want of air, and would be alone. Leave me, leave me—all—I pray you go !

> [*She staggers to a chair which is placed for her in* C.

LAR. (*officiously*). A sudden indisposition ails our muse. Gentlemen, stand aside, I beg. A fan !—a pouncet-box for the Countess !

FRED. Be it so. Remember, Countess von Thürenau, in case of need, that Frederick has but two friends—you and Voltaire. (*Takes* VOLTAIRE'S *arm.*) Come, Voltaire. Gentlemen, follow me.

VOL. She, too, 's been playing with fire, and burnt her fingers. Hot-headed girl !

LAR. (*aside to* ERFURT). Did you hear him ? That's plain speaking, at all events.

ERF. (*aside to him*). A diploma of favourite, signed and sealed. (*To* JULIAN.) Well, sir, you regret your heat of a few moments since. Have we unbound your eyes ?

JUL. Who begged light of you ? Better darkness than the pale-green light of deadly fens.

ERF. Count ! Another insult.

JUL. I have already said that I await your orders.

ERF. My friends shall be with you within the hour.

> [*All exeunt.* JULIAN *is following.*

THEC. (*on the chair*). Count Julian, stay. Stay, I say. I wish it. I stoop to beg of you. Well, Julian ! Blind fortune makes us meet once more to-night, though to-morrow only was to have cast the die. Perchance the gods are kinder than they seem, and would save us hours of suspense. One question. One single word as answer. Speak. Are you also blind?

JUL. Am I not to believe my eyes?

THEC. (*rising*). Not always, Julian. Circumstances are ofttimes as lying to the eye as to the ear. He falters. Oh, bitter destiny! His gold is counterfeit. His metal's no better tempered than that of other men.

JUL. You do well to rail, lady. Reproaches sit lightly on your lips.

THEO. Listen to me. Were one to come to me and say, "Count Julian, the man you love"—for I do love you—"is a coward, a vile wretch, whose name is thick stained with mire; he drags his fouled scutcheon in the dust; is but a bravo, who sells his sword to whoso will buy the notched and rusty blade," I should answer, "It is not true; it is a lie!"

JUL. I was prepared to say as much of you ten moments since. I believed in you with all my soul. Then that accursed door opened, and——

THEC. It was not enough. Were I to see you grovelling—ground into the dust—under a foe's point, imploring, for bare charity, a little life,—were my eyes to look on you gaming in a hell with loaded dice, I should murmur to myself, content in spirit, thus was he compelled to act. Such is my love—such my faith, patient and long-suffering, without which love is of no worth at all!

JUL. No. You would not endure coldly, as you profess, if you feel as deeply as you pretend to feel. When the Fates point with so direct a finger, you could not but believe.

THEC. (*impatiently*). The Fates! the Fates! Does your heart say nothing?

JUL. If my heart spoke after that I've seen, I'd tear it from my bosom with these hands.

THEC. A boast worthy of unstable faith. The low brute courage of the suicide, no more.

JUL. Madam!

THEC. Yes, low and vile. As low and vile as all this idle searching into a woman's secrets. As mean as this banding together of self-righteous men to hound her down. Strange it should need the hands of so many heroes to flush a woman's brow with shame. Truly a noble pastime, worthy of the gods! I knew they were there, the flight of evil birds, but thought not to find the eagle couched among them.

JUL. When you appeared, I had turned to go, too haughty to assume a part that lowered me in my own esteem—too proud to admit of a suspicion which profaned the lady of my love. You are so beautiful, I could not believe that Heaven had writ its name upon your face and blurred it from your heart. But I was deceived. Better, perchance, that I should know it now, for I have unveiled——

THEC. (*bitterly*). The truth! Say the word, as you believe it. But how know you that you are not victim of a misconception— fooled by a false fire, such as leads hinds through bogs to their despair?

JUL. Explain your conduct, if you can. I only ask to be convinced.

THEC. Count Julian, no! Remember our converse on this very spot but a few hours past—a time that seems now, alas, so long—so long ago! I said that the love which I demanded must be crowned with infinite faith. Since then you have doubted. Henceforth you are a stranger to me, and to a stranger I will not explain myself. What! A life of petty jealousies, of small quarrels, and puny pardonings? Fie! A life for water-carriers and market-wenches, but a life-long disgraceful chain to you and me. No, Count Julian; the book is closed, its clasps clamped-to for ever.

JUL. Your assumed anger, Thecla, deceives me not. The farce is well played, but is unworthy of you. The obscure lover falls into the shade before a conqueror of kings. How poor appears the conquest of one solitary heart when an entire people are prepared to worship at your feet! Frederick's greatness needed but a tangible glory mid his host to lead his arms from victory to victory. In truth, thrice happy king— thrice happy——

THEC. Count, peace! No more! You know not what you say!

JUL. (*fiercely*). Do I not? Have I not heard your name tossed, like a bubble on the air, in sport, by those who should have named you on their knees? Have I not seen you pointed at with nods and curlings of the lip, like any wanton woman of the town? For shame!

THEC. Count Julian!

JUL. Aye, I speak of that I know. You reap the harvest which you sowed unwittingly. I told you there were battles a. woman durst not wage without a smirching of her innocence. I told you that, in the unequal fight, you must inevitably be broken and undone. What are you now, who sit on the crazy throne of popular caprice? A beauteous lily, plucked from fostering earth, deprived of root, and so of life, placed in a gilded glass. After an hour's triumph, the flower will blacken and decay, spite of the gold that hems it round. Oh, Thecla! are you content that such should be your fate? Believe me, you 've mistaken the way; turn back, while yet there 's time. Come, rouse thee, Thecla! You may yet do something with your sullièd life. Remedy the follies of the past; blot out the errors of inexperienced youth. You said, with truth, "Our book is closed; its clasps are clamped for ever." Farewell! We meet no more! [*Exit.*

[THECLA *looks after him, clasps her hands over her eyes, then falls on the marble seat under statue. (Music as in First Tableau.)*

THEC. Gone! Gone, with bitter words and burning lip! Another vanished dream; another illusion lost? Alone, poor heart; ever alone! If *he* prove faithless, what, then, is true? The smile of Heaven, which warms and gives us life, 's a lie. The bursting spring, that heralds forth eternity, is but a mocking shade! This rose, which he begged but now, blooms still, despite his lack of faith. [*She clasps the feet of the statue.*] Oh, Love, Love, Love! wise were they of old who portrayed thee veiled. Thy form embodies the godliness of youth. Thy glorious feet are wet with dewy daffodils. Thy breath is fragrant as morning flowers. But 'neath that rainbow film there lurks a skull, from whose sightless orbs darts forth a lurid flame, that scorches and devours! Alone for evermore!

[*She lays her head upon the statue's feet. N.B. In the country, where the statue is, of course, painted on the flat, the pedestal must project several inches, to allow* THECLA *to rest head and arms on it, and be of a convenient height to allow of a graceful pose while sitting in abandonment.*

Enter VOLTAIRE, *down steps, without seeing her.*

VOL. I have taken hasty leave of Frederick, who was by no means pleased. I'm sick of embassies—the puppets are too easily moved. The only creature I regret to leave is Thecla. With the spirit of a will-o'-the-wisp, her heart is wrought in gold; but I much dread it may become tarnished here. It's no affair of mine. I'm getting a bad habit of meddling in others' lives. Since I took up diplomacy, I've forgotten how to think. It's plain I must make a choice—artist or ambassador. Of the two, I much prefer the artist.

THEC. (*raising slightly her head without changing her pose*). And you do well, Voltaire.

VOL. Here still, Thecla, at this hour! So pale and worn! Go in; the night air is damp.

THEC. (*sitting up*). Yes; art is the true life—the spring of great emotions, of noble impulses, of generous enthusiasm. I have thought it long; now conviction speaks plainly in my breast. (*Rises and comes forward.*) Art is the faithful friend whose placid smile shines on the soul alike in good and evil fortune, soothing with tenderness your every grief, gilding with poetry your every joy. Art is the real life.

VOL. (*takes snuff*). Cant phrases, my child, cant phrases, false as sea murmurs in a shell, happily adopted by the world, because we poets have shouted them aloud, and it's easier to accept others' opinions than form new ones for ourselves. I, who stand here, and I ought to know, wrote my best tragedies comfortably seated in a soft arm-chair, with a plentiful supply of the best rappee, chewing the cud of breakfast while awaiting dinner, my wig unruffled by fine poetic frenzy. Depend upon it, the public, moved to tears, are far more real poets than we who pump the water from their eyes. But never breathe to the simple public that great truth, or farewell enthusiasm—an absurd but necessary evil—farewell celebrity; worse still, farewell the ducats that chirp in our pockets and help to round our forms.

THEC. It's false, Voltaire, and you know it. Yourself live ofttimes in another world, are agitated by emotions which tear and inspire the soul. Were it not so, the spark would die in you, and you would sink dumb to insignificance. With all artists—with actors—'tis the same. I myself saw Garrick in London after Hamlet. He was pale. He trembled still, convulsed with the horrors of his mimic destiny. His aspect terrified me. I asked him if he needed help. "I am ill," he said. "This fever, every night renewed, slowly gnaws away my life. What matter! Though the frail body die, the soul's immortal!" From that day, Voltaire, I have longed for the larger life! I have burned to live in the grand joys and sorrows of the great ones of the past!

VOL. Thecla, you rave.

THEC. To be lulled into an enchanted world! To be borne far away from this narrow, sordid life! To commence each night a new existence—young, ardent, free! To burn with love and noble wrath, or bow with the heroism of self-sacrifice! To cause other hearts to beat with the whirl of your own passions! To make other eyes to weep with your own tears! Oh! Is not that to live? (*pensively*). There, too, might I not find forgetfulness?

VOL. Is this the haughty beauty, all smiles and triumphs, whom silly men choose to dub the favourite? Child, put this mad notion from you. Believe me, bury it at any cost. Garrick played upon your faith in him. To be able to tear yourself each night with passion you must be cold and calculating, you must be disillusioned, or you will die. You, Thecla, most certainly would die.

THEC. And you, who admit death as a possible result, would deny the power of art?

VOL. Play of muscles—combination of colour—effect of light. Delightful, no doubt, but nothing more. Self-willed that you are, you think me but a wind-bag. Would you have a proof? Crébillon writes to me from Paris that the great Lemaure, idol of the public, the reigning toast, has suddenly abdicated from her throne, still young, still steeped to the lips in plaudits. What think you of that? Do people wilfully give up the real life? It vexes me much, moreover, personally, as I counted specially on her for my 'Semiramis.'

THEO. Your 'Semiramis'? The tragedy you read to me. Who has taken her post?

VOL. No one as yet. The inspector of Paris theatres tears his wig, buffets the powder in his eyes in vain. The king rages, wont attend council, or see a minister. The Pompadour is furious. But time passes as I gossip here, and I must start to-night.

THEO. Voltaire, you seek an actress? I offer one—myself.

[VOL. *takes snuff—a pause.*

VOL. Eh! You! Poor child, your brain is overwrought.

THEO. Why so? As reigning sibyl, I have oft recited. here, and have drawn tears when I recked not if they smiled or wept. Not a word—no arguments—no counsellings. 'T were vain. I have thought of all, see all, know all. My will is strong; I will fight and conquer. Voltaire, are you my friend?

VOL. Am I—who knows? Some say I'm only a wicked old cynic; how, then, can I believe in friendship?

THEO. Old friend, long years have proved you.

VOL. Now she would wheedle me. Oh! woman, how artless, yet how deep!

THEO. Will you propose me? Yes, or no? Answer, quick!

VOL. Humph!

THEO. No time for humphs! Quick—yes, or no?

VOL. And if I refuse?

THEO. Then I will propose myself.

VOL. Pause on the threshold of this mad idea. Accept advice not often tendered. You will be unhappy.

THEO. Not more wretched then than now.

VOL. Be responsible for yourself then. I wash my hands. I will propose you.

THEO. When do you start?

VOL. In an hour.

THEO. We will go together.

VOL. Impossible. The silken chains which bind you to the world, to your family, to the Court?

THEO. Are broken, all!

VOL. I could have sworn that nothing could surprise me. I

was mistaken. You may become a great actress, Thecla; probably you will. But the art you worship will cost you tears of blood.

THEC. ˙Lend me your tablets. Write. This day, the 12th of June, 1746, Thecla Herfland, Countess of Thürenau died.

VOL. (*laughing, and throwing himself on a seat*). Amen! Though I don't understand a word!

THEO. Give me the pencil — turn another page. (*Writes. Music as in First Tableau to the end.*)—"I, at the point of death, do hereby will and bequeath my houses and estates, and all my wealth, to my dear sister, Olivia, Princess of Novgorod, absolutely, with the exception of a legacy of five hundred florins yearly to each of my two tirewomen, and a further sum of ten thousand florins of gold, which shall be paid, year by year, to M. de Voltaire, to be dispensed by him according to instructions given by me. Signed this 12th of June, 1746. Thecla von Thürenau." The name I've borne through good or ill report I look on for the last time. A strange feeling, old friend, is death in life.

VOL. But what would you do?

THEC. Live to love.

VOL. I begin to understand. That sum of ten thousand florins?

THEC. Is to be the annual pension of the greatest actress in France. The step is taken from which there's no return. The Countess von Thürenau is dead! May her memory yet linger for a little while shrined in a few faithful hearts! See to that paper at once, Voltaire. My women are to be trusted; they will arrange the rest. Who could have thought that Julian's words would so soon have borne their fruit! And now, to cast the veil of labour over my sullied past. Art shall light my path, a goal of lambent flame. Art and love must be the twin chords whose music shall give life to my new-born soul.

VOL. Thecla, I was wrong, and I recant. There does exist a mystic power. The sacred light shines forth in you, a prophetic promise that you shall be great.

THEC. Great! Yes. I *shall* be great! I *will* be great for him—and he shall learn to love me truly yet—despite the world.

      [*Curtain. Music as in First Tableau to the drop of curtain.*

PART II.

TABLEAU III.—*Drawing-room, in Palace of Versailles, lit up. Doors* R. L. *and* C. *Window in flat. When applause is heard, it is to be audible through the* CENTRE *door, which is supposed to lead to the Court Theatre. Card-table* R. *When scene opens,* ERFURT *and* LAROQUE *are playing at chess, seated on two chairs which have their backs to each other, with a stool in centre which holds chess-board.* ERFURT *sitting on horseback across his chair, elbows resting on its back.* LAROQUE *seated sideways on his chair, his arms over the back. When they abandon their game, they will move back the chairs and stool, and place chess-board on a table.*

LAR. (*moving a piece*). The world is not much larger than this chess-board after all, Baron. We are for ever bidding long farewells, and parting in tears only to come together unexpectedly at the very next turn. A tiny ball set in infinite space. This day five years ago we parted abruptly at Berlin, and here we are re-united at Versailles.

ERF. Yes, M. Laroque. Time for the moment is annihilated. Here we are quietly playing chess, as we did at Sans Souci five years ago.

LAR. When I was arrested.

ERF. Consequent on too pungent an epigram on His Most Sacred Majesty. I can't help smiling when I think of it. It was most laughable. Ha, ha !

LAR. I don't agree with you. Pray don't remind me of it, Baron. I feel a sort of crawling when I so much as think of prison-cells. A bed of stone—rats and spiders without end—and mildewed bread to eat ! Ugh ! But I've profited by the lesson, and have never so much as turned the smallest epigram since.

ERF. Nor an ode to the back of Venus or the frown of Jove?

LAR. Never ! No. Funerals now afford me a chaste emolument. They're more decorous ; besides, dead men don't sign orders of arrest. I have taken to serious literature, indite a graceful elegy sometimes, compose heart-rending tragedies. Moreover, you will easily understand that the dignity of my new position——

G

ERF. By-the-bye, I had forgotten to congratulate you. Since your rather hurried—ahem !—pardon me. Since your return to your native land you have been named, I think ?——

LAR. Governor of the Royal Theatres, Manager of His Majesty's Servants, and Inspector of Ballets. And a very difficult post I do assure you it is ! What has Time done for you, Baron ?

ERF. In the humdrum order of things, I have risen to the rank of Colonel, and am now attached to the Special Envoy sent to patch up a peace between France and Prussia.

LAR. Excuse me—let us steer clear of politics, an unwise pursuit of which by mere spectators leads often to the spiders and prison fare. You understand me. Besides, it scarcely suits the dignity of my new position——

ERF. I apologize ; check to your king.

LAR. What think you of our French Court ?

ERF. Charming ! Such balls ! such merrymakings ! such dainty ladies in such gay costumes ! such amorous dallyings ! More like a dream than a reality.

LAR. Only arrived but a few short hours since ; are you already launched ? Young heads ! young hearts ! So burning hot ! As Voltaire says, You'd disappear in steam but for the cold shower of sorrow. Come ; what fair ladies do you already know ?

ERF. Only two as yet. Both delightful, with the added pickle of just a little spite. Madame de Pierrefitte and the Duchess of Valence. Tell me about them ; who are they ?

LAR. Young man, I have the honour to repeat that my pastime lies in funerals, which afford a delectable addition to my income. Now these ladies are very much alive indeed, powerful at Court, and therefore dangerous. So I may only discourse to you concerning their virtue, which is long since dead and buried.

ERF. Checkmate.

LAR. I am beaten. Enough of chess (*they rise*). I remarked to you that our globe is small. You will find many here whom you already know.

ERF. Indeed ? But it's according to the teaching of our new philosophy. Many of us were born under one star, and our lives are compelled to move together in one cycle to the end.

LAR. As you are a new comer, I will venture on a word of advice. The mystic opinions in vogue at Frederick's Court are not the fashion here. Under the rosy auspices of the Pompadour we sing and dance and feast, and trouble ourselves concerning Reason not at all !

ERF. Yet Voltaire is here ?

LAR. Yes, but given over to the drama now, rather than to abstruse mysticism.

ERF. Why the drama?

LAR. Because the railer has been taken in the toils. He is tied to the triumphal car of our great actress here, and by her is softened into quite another man. Yes, you will find old friends in plenty. Yesterday was presented at Court the new Ambassadress from Russia. Judge of my surprise when I beheld that marble paragon, the Princess of Novgorod.

ERF. She! Scarce suited to this laughing Court.

LAR. The Princess Olivia never was more imposing and severe. Pale, serious, clad in deepest sable—for she still wears mourning for her sister—she dropped among us rather like an iceberg than a thunderbolt. King Louis dared not look her in the face. The Duke de Richelieu seemed quite modest and abashed. Passing by the Pompadour, she flung at her a stony glance, which would have sent Medusa mad with jealousy, as though to say, "See what a great wall there is betwixt us two!" Recognizing me, her thoughts reverted to her dead sister, and she buried her features in her handkerchief. Excellent, tender-hearted creature!

ERF. Poor, erring Northern Muse! She always was a thorn in the Princess's side.

LAR. Apropos of Thecla, we have here an actress of remarkable talent—the same whose shadow is Voltaire—whose oddity is as strange as is her genius.

ERF. I know! Mademoiselle Fidès.* Her fame has reached Berlin; and I have special orders from Frederick to write to him of her. This very night, I'm told, she's to declaim. . I'm longing to see her.

LAR. Yes—in the Court Theatre, presently. Prepare yourself for a great surprise. Does your philosophy, which tells of people born under one star, say anything of those who are cast in the same mould? The new genius is the living image of poor Countess Thecla, whose sudden death at the ball of Sans Souci shocked us so much five years ago. The same voice, the same figure, the same bright, animated smile. The first time I saw her, I stood with goggle eyes and open mouth, unable to articulate a word, which drew from her rosy lips a peal of laughter. Indeed, had we not all assisted at the grand obsequies of the late Countess,—on which, by the way, I wrote so excellent an ode——

ERF. Such coincidences of feature are by no means rare. We all know cases of mistaken identity.

LAR. But this resemblance, I tell you, is prodigious.

* Better make the actors pronounce it Spanish fashion—Fee-dez.

Enter MADAME DE PIERREFITTE *and* DUCHESS DE VALENCE,
arm in arm.

MAD. DE P. (*threatening bombastically with fan.*) What! do
you dare to gossip here, oh, recreant scions of a worthy race?
To-morrow, at cock-crow, ye shall be broken on the wheel, and
your ashes scattered by the common executioner.

DUCH. (*the same business*). You shall be burned alive, by
express orders of the Pompadour. I'm not certain you shan't
first be pilloried.

LAR. Mercy, ladies, mercy. You crush us to the earth. Of
what fearful enormity are we innocently guilty?

MAD. DE P. Of the gravest crime possible at the Court of
France in the year of grace in which we live.

DUCH. High treason, oh, hardened criminals! You dare
quietly to abuse your neighbours here, when the last new wonder
of the world—the priceless pearl of the Comédie Française—is
making her triumphant entry into the grand saloon! Sinners,
feel ye no remorse?

ERF. Mademoiselle Fidès has arrived?

LAR. We were speaking but now of her.

MAD. DE P. And pray of what other subject could you speak?
In the circle of the Pompadour, in the King's private chamber,
even at Richelieu's naughty little suppers, in the public street,
there is but one matter of discourse — all trumpet forth one
name. It's sickening.

DUCH. The celebrated actress beguiles generals into forgetting
war, reverend ministers into cropping short their sermons; more
marvellous still, for she has a dreadful will of her own, she
refuses to act in tragedies of the most colossal excellence. Did
she not decline to act in a play of yours, dear Madame de Pierrefitte?

MAD. DE P. It matters not, dear Duchess, if she did.

LAR. And has she not conquered the invincible Julian of
Toledo, who, because he's rude, and turns up his eyes, and wears
black clothes, all the ladies adore?

DUCH. (*tapping him with fan*). Hush! Don't speak of him
before our dear friend here. She is herself stricken, makes
mad love to him, follows him like a pet dog, bows meekly
beneath his sarcasms, and he brushes her from him as though
she were a fly! Ha, ha!

ERF. What! is he, too, at Versailles?

MAD. DE P. Count Julian? Yes; as minister from Spain.
Do you know him, Baron?

ERF. Five years ago, at Berlin, he pinked me with his sword.

DUCH. Oh, how delightful! A duel about a woman.

ERF. Who was not worth the blood we spilt. He's a strange man who strives to carry poetry into the realities of life, instead of studying philosophy.

MAD. DE P. At any rate, his manner's not poetical towards the Pompadour! The Puritan declines even to be presented to her—think of that!

DUCH. Which so piques her woman's vanity, that she's for ever making advances to him underhand.

LAR. The which he rejects with horror and scorn! A strange man, indeed!

MAD. DE P. And he's a poet too. Has written a glorious tragedy, called 'Sappho.' I have learnt much of it by heart.

(*Sighs.*)

LAR. Yes, 'Sappho'; in which Mademoiselle Fidès is so great.

MAD. DE P. Great, indeed! For my part, I can't see the woman's talent which drives you men so crazy.

ERF. But who is this woman? Whence does she come? Fidès is not a name.

MAD. DE P. No. She's a mystery, and therefore the more enchanting. Her name, I'm told, means *faith*. She's said to be daughter of a gipsy—sister to a galley-slave—at all events, something of very ignoble birth.

DUCH. And, let's whisper, her house is said to be a Mahomet's paradise; the very centre and summit of all that's rare and elegant and deliciously sinful in all gay Paris.

MAD. DE P. Oh, the goings-on in that divine retreat! It's murmured that she plays Aspasia there to at least a dozen Alcibiades'!

DUCH. I vow it makes me blush! It's certain that her fortune is immense—how acquired?

DUCH. 〉
MAD. DE P. 〉 Ah! how acquired?

[*Both nod in unison and hide faces behind fans.*

LAR. The dignity of my position forbids my listening to such scandal. Moreover, I must visit the stage, and see that all's prepared. Ladies, I take my leave. [*Exit.*

MAD. DE P. That dear Laroque. He, at least, ought to be devoted to her. She feathers his nest for him with gold. He had the honour of bringing her out.

DUCH. No. She owes all to her worshipper, Voltaire, who prepared her triumph in Semiramis. But here he comes.

Enter VOLTAIRE.

MAD. DE P. Well, you bad old man. We were just saying wicked things of you.

VOL. (*kissing her hand*). So I should have thought, fair lady. I only *think* wicked things of you.

DUCH. (*laughing*). Well said, Voltaire! 'Twere wiser, dear Madame, not to array your arms against so formidable an enemy.

MAD. DE P. (*haughtily*). I am not afraid of him. Love will leave him very little time for war.

VOL. Keep your mosquito stings for others, ladies. They harm me not. I marvel, really, that grand and noble dames like you should waste so much ribald curiosity on a poor actress, who is a daughter to me in my increasing age. It is hard, no doubt, for you to pardon her beauty, her spirits, and her genius——

MAD. DE P. You say nothing of her spotless name.

VOL. Because she is, indeed, so pure, that it is, doubtless, difficult for you even to comprehend the prodigy.

DUCH.
MAD. DE P. } Oh, oh, oh!

Enter LAROQUE, *hurriedly.*

LAR. Ladies, for pity's sake, lend me a smelling-bottle—a pouncet-box.

MAD. DE P. Good gracious! what's the matter? You seem quite overcome.

LAR. Mademoiselle Fidès has fainted.

DUCH. Is that all? The gipsies have come to take her away.

MAD. DE P. The galley-slave brother has probably appeared. Really, these repeated tumblings about of hers are simply nauseating.

VOL. Fainted! and yet she was well but now. Tell us more, Laroque.

LAR. As you know, in a moment of caprice she had donned the habit of a fortune-teller, and was moving about the grand saloon, prophesying good or evil to those around, when suddenly she came to the Princess of Novgorod. Startled by her mourning or her stony presence, she turned deadly pale, staggered, and would have fallen had I not placed her in a chair. All gave what help they could, but she's now in strong hysterics.

VOL. How rash! how rash!—would she betray herself?

[*Exit, hastily.*

MAD. DE P. I wonder she can't invent something newer than these fainting fits.

LAR. (*seeing wine, glasses, &c., on table at side*). Ah! here's water. [*Exit with glass.*

MAD. DE P. But there's always something touching in feeble health, dear Duchess. Let us leave off rouge, and paint ourselves black under the eyes. Would it be becoming?

VOL. (*enters*). It's over, and she's said nothing.

ERF. Is she subject to these attacks?

VOL. Yes; she's not strong, is most excitable, and in the past has suffered much.

DUCH. Of course, with a gipsy father to beat one till one cries!

MAD. DE P. And a galley-slave brother to slap one black and blue!

VOL. Bless your kind hearts, sweet ladies. Most painful! For *she* didn't deserve it. *You* have no brothers, I think? Sometimes, from the intoxication and triumph of the present, her mind wanders back to the disappointments of the past, and then she's no longer mistress of herself. I've seen her break down sometimes whilst acting, as if her strength had left her suddenly.

ERF. Which, of course, brings the performance to an untimely close.

MAD. DE P. Oh dear, no. How innocent you are! Therein lies the consummate artfulness. Her friends spread, with long faces, the distressing news. Fidès has had a fit! The poor, dear, guileless public believes, admires, and melts in pity. Second announcement: Fidès will endeavour to recite. A grateful murmur of applause. Up flies the curtain—the actress appears, pale, scarcely able to stand. A general hurrah! Some begin to cry. Tears are catching; soon the house is white with pocket-handkerchiefs. A dead silence as she breathes forth some feeble words. Her pallor gives place to a hectic flush!—febrile energy in the public service. Enthusiasm rises to delirium. "Out with her horses, and let us drag her home!" That's the way she made her reputation, the cunning minx.

VOL. Madame, unsay those false and cruel words. Yet it's what experience of human nature has led me to expect. (*To the Duchess.*) If I were to relate, Duchess, what a power of heaven-born inspiration hangs around her lips,—how, tossed on the sea of passion, her convulsed fingers tear her tender skin under the folds of her Greek robe,—(*Duchess laughs. He turns to the other*),—did I explain to you that, were the whirl of her impetuous energy not consumed by the exigencies of her art, she must go mad——

MAD. DE P. (*laughing*). Ha, ha! a little lunacy would make it quite complete! How terribly in earnest, M. de Voltaire!

VOL. Do you ladies then believe in nothing?

MAD. DE P. In nothing (*curtsying*), and M. de Voltaire has been our master.

VOL. Ladies, this is basest calumny. I must seek safety in flight, or I shall end by blushing for myself as well as you!

[*Exit.*

DUCH. We've put him to flight. Fancy a philosopher in love! How deliciously new!

ERF. The grand saloon is crowded with guests. Will you come, ladies?

MAD. DE P. No. The theatre opens later, and the grand hall's insufferably hot. Here are cards and dice. Suppose we remain in the cool awhile, and play. What shall it be? Anything to pass the time. Lansquenet?

DUCH. By all means, Lansquenet. Baron Erfurt, will you join us in a game?

ERF. With pleasure. (*They sit.* MADAME DE PERREFITTE *and* DUCHESS *on either side.* ERFURT *in centre.*) Here's fifty louis for the pool. Queen of Hearts! Then it's for you, Duchess, to deal.

Enter NOVGOROD, *leading in his wife, pale, in black.*

NOV. Compose yourself, madame, and remember who you are; if not for your own sake, at least for mine. I tell you it was a trick of your overheated imagination.

OLIV. No. I repeat to you that it was *her* voice,—the voice, as well as the features, of my dead sister, Thecla.

NOV. Nonsense. I warned you beforehand of the extraordinary likeness existing between the actress and the late Countess of Thürenau.

OLIV. But it was not alone the likeness, though that chilled my veins. Her hand was cold, and held mine long in hers.

NOV. What's this I hear? Have we come to this? Did the low player dare contaminate the hand of the Princess of Novgorod? And you permitted it?

OLIV. I tell you it is either Thecla or her ghost returned to earth.

NOV. Your brain wanders. Once more, compose yourself, or people will be asking the cause of your emotion. Remember, too, that, as happily she's dead, no one need know that she was united to us by ties of blood. Both Voltaire and Laroque have promised to be silent.

OLIV. Yet, husband, admit for an instant that it might be she. Could Thecla return to life—

NOV. I tell you she *cannot*. Her ashes moulder in the family resting-place of Herfland; a decent monument recites her virtues and her early death. In natural course, we inherited from her, very right and proper, and so there's an end. Peace be with her soul.

OLIV. Yet my mind misgives me.

NOV. Obey my will. Would you wish to share the slur upon her name? Would you desire hers always to be united

publicly to yours—to mine? Compose yourself, I say, and hold
your peace. [*She bows her head.*

OLIV. Be it as you will.

ERF. And he, too, is smitten with the actress. Certainly the
superb Count Julian is unlucky in his loves.

DUCH. Did we not hear rumours of something romantic
long ago between him and your hair-brained Countess of
Thürenau?

ERF. Yes. He grieved deeply for her death, accused himself
of murder, attired himself in black, and swore to remain faithful
to her memory.

MAD. DE P. I hate that Countess of Thürenau!

DUCH. You never saw her, dear.

MAD. DE P. No matter, my love. How exasperating are
these Spaniards with their romance. Faithful to a shade!

DUCH. There's no such powerful rival as the dead.

MAD. DE P. And such a shade! Absurd! A sort of courtesan of high degree decked out with poetry, like gingerbread
gilded for a fair.

NOV. (*aside to Olivia*). You hear them?

ERF. Hush. That lady there in black is the Princess of
Novgorod.

NOV. They observe us, Princess; be calm, and raise your
head.

ERF. Her sister, but one of a much nobler stamp.

DUCH. Whose sister?

ERF. Hush! The Countess Thecla's. Let us change the
subject.

MAD. DE P. I am not obliged to know it.

DUCH. Nor I. And such an odious woman, too!

ERF. But, ladies, think of me.

MAD. DE P. You need not see her. Look the other way.
I should dearly like to wound this overpowering pride.

DUCH. And so should I. (*Aloud.*) About this said departed
Lady Thecla, rumour whispered the most marvellous things.
There were really the most improper stories—quite dreadful—
such as I could not possibly repeat.

MAD. DE P. Easily led astray, they say, poor thing. But
then she was half-witted, and should have been shut up. What-
ever her family were about, I can't think. Perhaps her sister
was no better than she.

DUCH. There you're wrong, dear—really too severe. I'm
told the sister was a perfect stone, while the Lady Thecla—well,
was quite the contrary. Hid her vices under a mask of poetry.
Everything's permitted to genius. Don't you wish you were a
genius, dear?

H

Enter THEOLA, *masked and dressed as a fortune-teller, on*
LAROQUE'S *arm.*

THEC. (*pauses and overhears conversation a short while*). She
listens, impassive and indifferent! without one word for the
sister who is gone!

MAD. DE P. (*turning to* NOVGOROD). By-the-bye, Prince, you
have been ambassador at Berlin. Did you know her?

NOV. Who?

MAD. DE P. The Countess of Thürenau.

NOV. (*confused, looking at* OLIVIA *and* LAROQUE). Ahem!
Certainly not, madame. The Prince of Novgorod knows no
ladies of questionable reputation.

DUCH. Indeed. Most exemplary. I congratulate you, Prince.

THEC. (*restraining herself no more, and coming impetuously
forward*). Princess of Novgorod, defend your sister's name from
calumny.

MAD. DE P. (*feigning surprise*). *Her* sister!

LAR. (*uneasily*). The dignity of my position forbids that I should
compromise myself. I smell rats and spiders in the wind! [*Exit.*

THEO. Princess, have you nothing in answer to these bitter
tongues?

OLIV. (*surprised, then coldly*). I may pity her fate, but I may
not defend her.

THEO. 'Tis she who speaks!

DUCH. Really, Prince—too distress'd, I'm sure.

[*They rise from card-table.*

MAD. DE P. Truly grieved that we—

NOV. (*embarrassed*). Ladies, say no more. My opinion of her
was always the same as yours. One who can drag an ancestral
title in the dust is worthy of odium and contempt. Thecla von
Thürenau was no relation of mine, was no longer the sister of
my wife; for we had both denied and cast her off. Was it not
so?—answer, Olivia.

OLIV. (*after a pause, in a broken voice*). Yes!

THEC. (*aside*). Oh, degraded souls! steeped in the slime of
utter selfishness! (*Aloud.*) Did not this lost one at the point
of death bequeath to you her splendid revenues? You did not
then, I think, deny the ties of blood?

NOV. Who are you who, concealed beneath a mask, dare thus
to speak to me?

THEC. (*in anger and emotion*). Who am I? I—

NOV. Who?

VOLTAIRE *enters behind, and lays his hand on her arm.*

VOL. Mademoiselle Fidès, of the Comédie Française.

ERF. The great actress!

Nov. The vile player!—sprung from some prison spawn. Ha! ha! I was wrong to be incensed, though it's strange that such creatures are admitted here! You may, if you will, recite to my scullions in the kitchen to-morrow. It will amuse them, and you shall be well paid.

Vol. (*aside*). My child—patience—have a care.

Theo. Never fear, old friend. Yes, Prince of Novgorod, I am the player, present here by His Majesty's desire. We both are players, you and I. But you are always tricked out and painted for the boards, whilst I act only at night. The part you play is ever the same—false, hypocritical, woven in untruth; baser than prison spawn, in that your god has always been yourself.

Nov. Were you not a woman, I'd have you whipped at the cart's tail for this—

Theo. Insolent!

Vol. Prince, you forget yourself.

Nov. Aye, whipped! In the public market-place, as warning to her fellows!

> [*Raises his glove to strike her,* Julian *enters, comes down between them, and takes glove from his hand.*

Nov. Count of Toledo!

Theo. (*aside, in joy*). He! at last!

Duch. This is amusing; quite an impromptu play.

Mad. de P. The Puritan Spaniard can warm, it seems, though marble to me. This woman's impudence is past belief.

Nov. I have been publicly insulted by one who is admitted here on sufferance. Public shall her punishment be. I'll see to it.

Jul. You will do nothing of the kind.

Nov. And who will prevent me, pray?

Jul. I.

Nov. You? Make common cause with this low scum! and against me, Prince of Novgorod? You, a Spanish nobleman?

Jul. I know not your cause of quarrel nor wish to be informed. I perceived a glove raised by a man against a woman, an act *not* worthy of praise even though she be a defenceless player; and as a man I saw my duty and did it, that is all.

Vol. This fellow almost reconciles me to my kind.

Nov. Beware, young sir. If you defend, you divide with her the insult.

Jul. As you please. Permit me to return your glove.

Mad. de P. He warms into life. His cheek is flushed. I feel I hate this woman.

Nov. Our official rank, sir, forbids a scandal. You shall answer for this insult before the King. Princess, your hand.

> [*They are going out, when* Theola *intercepts, and says aside to* Olivia,

THEC. Your idol is as insatiable as pitiless. You will sacrifice on its altar family and friends.

OLIV. (*starts*). Ha! (*Coldly.*) Woman, let me pass.

[*Exit* PRINCE *and* PRINCESS OF NOVGOROD.

ERF. (*to* MADAME DE PIERREFITTE). Did you remark? She withered her with a gorgon look.

MAD. DE P. I go to take my seat for the recital, or I shall lose favour with the Pompadour, and that means disgrace and frowns from His Majesty the King.

DUCH. And I follow your example, though, after this excitement, she's sure to have a fit, and I'm tired of them. Come.

MAD. DE P. Count Julian, are you with us? No! You wish your fortune told?

DUCH. (*aside*). Count, you are brave. May your quarrel not embroil you with His Majesty; but Russia is powerful, and France on the eve of war with Frederick. Believe me, it were wise to be well with the King's favourite. Fidès is her dearest friend. She may arrange it for you. Take my advice.

MAD. DE P. Come, dear Duchess. He loves this upstart. She had best not measure blades with me.

[*Exeunt* MAD. DE P., DUCHESS, *and* ERFURT.

VOL. Is it safe to leave them alone together? (THECLA *motions him away.*) Well, well. Have your will. It's no affair of mine. I am with you, ladies. [*Exit.*

THEC. Count, receive my thanks. You have not defended a dishonourable cause. The day may come when I can tell you more. And now, farewell; you have my gratitude.

[*Fausse sortie.*

JUL. Stay! one instant! Though you owe me nothing, yet I have a favour to beg. Your voice echoes far into the caverns of the past, sadly stirring the dry leaves of an imperishable sorrow. Raise for me that mask a moment. I have seen your face at a distance on the stage. I know your name. I would look upon you, and hear it from your lips.

THEC. An idle wish. (*Takes off mask ;* * *then, simply,*) They call me Fidès.

JUL. How passing strange! The same—yet, no. There is a veil of melancholy and deep-ploughed lines of suffering that other face, thank God, never wore. No, you are not the same.

THEC. (*gaily, with curtsey*). I am a humble fortune-teller; shall I tell you yours, my fine signior?

JUL. Whence would you draw your horoscope?

THEC. From the past.

JUL. What know you of the past?

* She need not put it on again.

THEC. Now you ask too much. Trust in the power of an ever-watchful spirit, hovering round and spying out your ways.

JUL. That you say lightly is a truth to me. For five years I've felt that there's, indeed, a spirit watching over me, whose mysterious presence wraps me round.

THEC. (smiling). We each have a guardian angel. So, at least, the poets tell us.

JUL. For five years I've sought in vain. But a still voice tells me now the spirit's near at hand.

THEO. (in mock tragic tones). And what gorgeous fretted palace-roof covers this intangible existence?

JUL. The painted canvas vault of the Comédie Française.

THEC. A strange lodging; but angels, they say, can perch anywhere. And by what name's your spirit called?

JUL. By a sweet name, as mystic as her nature, as harmonious as her voice. Her name is Faith; though why or how she works this charm is a mystery to me. Do you know her, lady?

THEC. Yes. But, like you, I fail to see how an angel in the guise of a poor actress——

JUL. Listen. By a favour which myself I should never have had the ambition to seek,—commissioned, too, by a minister who loves me not,—I was despatched a short time since on a special embassy to Paris. Arrived in France, I found a corrupt Court at the feet of a shameless courtesan. Not caring to conceal my contempt alike for court and favourite, I hurled my scorn at both. Hourly I waited for my passports, supposing I should be desired to leave; instead of which the Pompadour wrote to Spain, begging that I might be confirmed as plenipotentiary to France. Who interests the Pompadour in me in spite of my contempt? All this was strange. Finally, a few days back, I received a card, which bore the words, "Come to the Comédie Française," written in characters similar to many letters from time to time received—letters which spoke to me in accents of help and comfort that seemed to whisper from beyond the grave. I have an unknown protectress, a tender counsellor, but where? I went to the theatre; you were on the stage, playing the character of a high-souled woman misjudged through circumstances.

THEC. Wild phantasy. None of this points to me as your mysterious spirit.

JUL. There, before a thousand eyes that knew it not, took place a wondrous prodigy. There was the woman that I loved— whose untimely death has been the gnawing sorrow of my later life. No, not glamour. It seemed sober truth. By what magic did the tomb yawn before my sight? exposing a world long vanished and forgot, in the midst of which *she* moved — she

who, till too late, I never understood,—who died, perchance, for
me—whom I loved with a man's despotic love, whom I love yet
—the more that she was wrested from me. (*These broken sentences
must be spoken very fast.*)   [*Music as in other Tableaux.*

THEC. (*in increasing agitation*). Thanks, thanks, Heaven!
Now I am repaid!

JUL. I saw her yet again, purified by the pale corpse-lights of
the hidden world. From my shadowed corner I hung upon your
every movement, drank in your every smile. You brought back
the past to me in a hallowed present of diminished grief. In
you the irrevocable exists no more, for the relentless grave gives
up its dead. Fidès! see me kneel and bow myself in the dread
presence of a hope renewed.   [*Music.*

THEC. (*aside.*) Can *he* speak truth, who proved so unstable in
his faith? (*Aloud*) No. Your thoughts but linger round the
vanished dead, flecking with the sun of your own life that which
is past and gone. You see in me but the portrait of another.
No, Count; the low-born player might believe and hope who is
but mortal like the rest. Where would the future of the poor
actress be, if time taught you to see in her nothing but a mask?
No; there are griefs we can bear but once and live. In pity
pursue me not. Pass on your way—be merciful!   [*Music.*

JUL. Then 'tis indeed true? *Your* heart beats wildly as does
mine! Your blood flows surging in your veins like mine! You
burn with the same fever as devours me! You love me, Fidès!
I knew it. Oh, speak the words!

THEC. If such could be, I would exact the same deep love
you gave to her who's dead. Valued for myself alone I should
yet be jealous of these memories. Your imagination sees me
other than I really am. If you in truth so long have mourned,
best trim the cherished flames and sit by them.   [*Music.*

Enter LAROQUE.

LAR. Where's Mademoiselle Fidès? Quick. As you respect
my office, delay no more. The symphony's begun; the Court
all expectation.

THEC. I come. (*To* JULIAN.) Destiny has cut our speech.
Are we to knit it up again?

JUL. Yes! at any cost: Were I to follow you to your home—

THEC. Enough. You will receive a token from me presently.
(MAD. DE P. *appears at back*, R. " A token! Ah!" *and dis-
appears.*) See you interpret it aright.

LAR. (*at door*). Mademoiselle Fidès!

THEC. I come! Between the acts meet me here again. Then
—who knows what the angel may ordain? I *may* say to you,
" Julian, the flower of literature and art in France await me *there.*

The King, the Court, cultivated minds from many lands—more, the author of the play, Voltaire. I shall be stunned with plaudits, overwhelmed with wreaths and garlands. Yet for love of you am I prepared to break with all. I will leave my brilliant future for your sake. Together we will wander into a new world, and commence our lives afresh." Thus *may* I speak.

Jul. Casting the die of certain happiness.

Thec. Take heed that you can trust yourself. It may yet be, alas! that for myself you love me not. I bear the form of another sanctified to you by death. How know you that my soul speaks the same language as my face?

Lar. (*at door*). They wax impatient. For the love of Heaven, mademoiselle!

Thec. I come! I come! Till then adieu.

> [*She withdraws her hand from him, and exit with* Laroque.

Jul. What is this siren who has spun her web about my limbs? Thecla! she wears thy lineaments; I seek to trace thy soul in her! Forgive if now thou lookest down on me! The past lies here (*hand on breast*), and may never be effaced.

> [*Exit slowly after* Thecla.

Enter Madame de Pierrefitte *at back* R., *with a fan in her hand.*

Mad. de P. Gone! And he who vaunts so high his purity falls conquered by this Dălĭlăh of the boards. Oh, man! man! So has it ever been in the history of the world. Invincible to rude assaults. A bright eye suffused with tears, an ivory shoulder cunningly displayed, and you succumb, weighed down with chains of imitation gold!

Voltaire *enters.*

Vol. Heigho! I am fatigued. It is like bran in the mouth to hear people laugh at one's own jokes. Let others feed their ears, I'll e'en recruit my body with sleep. Ah! The Queen Regnant of the college of spite hatching some new mischief, I'll be bound. What a pity we can't seize the hive, and plunge it fathoms deep beneath the sea! But then might the age of Reason dawn, and we're not ripe for it. (*Aloud.*) Alone, madame, while the great actress declaims my favourite lines? A poor compliment to both of us.*

Mad. de P. I am not well, or etiquette would force me to be there. Besides, the Pompadour gave me her fan to change, and I must do the errand. This, it appears, is a favourite one, adorned with strange mottoes and cabalistic signs, too good for common

---

* Makes himself comfortable in an arm-chair.

use. It should be of value, it's so very ugly. And so you see I'm forced to play the Abigail.

Vol. You stoop preparing for a higher rise. I like to find prudent brains behind a comely face; for we see so little of ladies' faces now-a-days, that worship must hang on what's concealed beneath.

Mad. de P. M. de Voltaire, you are quite another man, or are you merely laying traps for us? You've ceased telling us unpleasant truths. You smile and hold your caustic tongue, wearing a quaint festive aspect, like some bear combed and bedizened for a show.

Vol. I admit I'm lost, and wander in a maze. We live in a world of idiots, whose inane applause sends cold shudders down my back, and of dames more bold and painted than the figure-heads of ships. And yet I dare not rail, for I've met just one or two who must have fluttered among us from some better sphere, shaking my faith in the scepticism of a life. When you lose your anchorage, even to unbelief, you're tossed and tumbled in a sea of troubles. I'm getting old.

Mad. de P. You're in your dotage, and this player girl will revenge us on you yet. (*He places handkerchief over his face.*) Aha! How sweet 'twill be to gibe at you when you gravely air a lowborn wife in the alleys of the park, surrounded by a crowd of baby cynics, more corkscrew-visaged than you are yourself.

Vol. (*under handkerchief*). Don't! The picture's harrowing in the extreme.

Mad. de P. (*waving her fan over him*). Awful retribution for him who so long has scourged our poor little sins.

Vol. The buzzing of insects soothes to slumber; but your babble takes away my breath, and reminds me that I came here for rest.

Mad. de P. While Fidès speaks the verses of the great Voltaire?

Vol. (*removing one corner of the handkerchief*). It is not lively to gaze on one's own plays. (*Aside.*) Wake me if you have anything charitable to say. That will secure me a good sound sleep.

[*Replaces handkerchief over face.*

Enter Servant *with silver salver, on which is a scrap of paper and a faded rose.*

Mad. de P. What's this? "For the Count of Toledo, from Mademoiselle Fidès," written in her hand. A withered flower, a musty love-token. Then they've known each other long, these modest love-birds! I seem to recognize your face?

SERV. Yes, madame. 'Twas thanks to your kindness I obtained service in the palace.

MAD. DE P. A withered flower! Starting, no doubt, a stream of pent-up remembrances! (*Aloud.*) I remember well. I who launched can aid in your career. The actress bade you give him this. *I* bid you carry this instead. (*Gives fan and takes flower.*) Return when he shall enter presently. Fifty louis if you do my will. One word, and the hand that raised can cast you down.

SERV. Madame, you shall be obeyed. [*Exit.*

VOL. (*withdrawing handkerchief*). What's that? I was dozing off. You spoke. Whose praises were you about to sing? (*Applause without.*) Aha! Fidès is surpassing herself. Go on. Clap your idle palms and bray forth your asinine approval. For once you're in the right. When I produced my finest works, and they rose like this at me, I answered them with jeers. But for her somehow there's music in the stamping of their foolish feet. I'm getting contaminated with their mud. Yet interest in another is not without its charm. There's something plea-sant—— You there, madame? I retract. I dreamed, and dreams run contrary to sober truth. Bravo! Clap on! clap on! She deserves it all. As I'm a living fool I must add my degene-rate self to all this folly. Brava! brava! See the sheep run where the bell-wether bleats.

[*Is running out. Bumps against* DUCHESS *and* ERFURT, *who enter.*

DUCH. M. de Voltaire!

VOL. Pardon. Not my fault. Merely the instinct of the silly sheep! Brava! [*Runs out.*

ERF. He's demented!

DUCH. Is the man failing in his intellect?

MAD. DE P. No matter. More harmless now that she has cut his claws.

DUCH. The Baron has seen and thinks her wonderful.

MAD. DE P. Did he weep? It's etiquette to weep at a Court performance.

ERF. Why so?

MAD. DE P. Because Fidès once drew a tear—one precious priceless pearly drop—from the eye of His Most Gracious Majesty; and ever since the Court has deemed itself obliged to weep like so many Niobes. They've made of our two theatres two great lakes, in which one might plunge and drown oneself.

Enter JULIAN.

DUCH. Here's Count Julian following the mode. See how pensive and how sad he looks. His face in mourning, like his dress. Have you, too, been weeping, noble Count? Then there's hope for you. We'll make a courtier of you yet.

MAD. DE P. The nameless gipsy has bewitched him.

Enter SERVANT, *with fan on salver.*

JUL. "For the Count of Toledo, from Mademoiselle Fidès." Give it me. The token she bade me interpret aright. May the protecting spirit not desert me. A fan, covered with inscriptions. Strange! What's this one which seems expressly turned to view.

> "Unless a man can mount he ne'er will rise;
> Timid, he'll not win smiles from ladies' eyes.
> Better to fall than brook the peasant's lot,
> To live unnoticed and to die forgot."

A singular enigma—at variance with her speech just now!

DUCH. A present from Mademoiselle Fidès? You are highly honoured, though a fan is hardly an appropriate gift to so valiant a gentleman as Count Julian.

MAD. DE P. A fan! May I admire it?

JUL. (*abstracted*). "Unless a man can mount he ne'er will rise." How in Heaven's name can this apply to me?

MAD. DE P. In all wide France there is but one fan like this, presented by His Majesty on her fête-day to the Pompadour.

DUCH. True. It is the same. I recognize it. What can it mean?

JUL. Ladies, you mistake. This present comes from Mademoiselle Fidès.

MAD. DE P. And this fan as certainly belongs to the Marquise de Pompadour.

DUCH. Who, perhaps, sent it through Mademoiselle Fidès for sundry *private* reasons. May it not mean an interview? O, fie! how deceitful is the world. (*Laughs behind her fan.*)

MAD. DE P. What delicacy it shows in her. A mask cast over the germs of an intrigue. (*Laughs behind her fan.*)

JUL. What do you mean?

DUCH. Hush! You may trust us. We're *very* discreet. Ha! ha! ha!

MAD. DE P. Let us congratulate you, Count, on your success.

DUCH. And the new star, after all, but plays the confidant. Ha, ha!

MAD. DE P. The great actress descends from her lofty pedestal. Ha, ha!

JUL. I call upon you to explain the meaning of your words.

[*Applause within.*

ERF. Ah! Mademoiselle Fidès begins her second scene!

DUCH. Then let us go. We must not lose a syllable. 'Tis the decree of fashion.

MAD. DE P. Yes. Let us go. Oh, for shame, Count! How dreadfully deep! Your secret's safe with us. Come, Baron; lead the way.

DUCH. So all this railing at the favourite was merely bluster.

MAD. DE P. His contempt for our frivolity but idle wind.

DUCH. Oh, fie! A heaven-born diplomat!

[Exeunt arm-in-arm, preceded by ERFURT.

JUL. What mean these nods and raisings of the brow? Fidès a pander to the Pompadour? Not possible. Yet how explain the favourite's interest in me? Can so much guile lurk 'neath so fair a front? Why speak of leaving the triumphs of the stage? Could she stoop to toy with my deep grief, whose voice was as balm upon my wounds? And this fan, with its strange legend. Alas! a likeness in feature, nothing more. Forgive me, Thecla, that I profaned thy memory.

[Sits at card-table, with back to the people on the stage, and buries face in hands. He had better leave fan on table.

LAR. (*entering*). Bravo! bravissimo! Nothing·could go better. The boxes are resplendent with lace and diamonds. Fidès outshines herself. Bless her great genius. . My prologue was not ineffective. His Majesty deigned to smile on me. Inspector of Ballets may lead to a yet higher post.

Enter OFFICER—*to* LAROQUE. Count Julian of Toledo?

LAR. (*drags him to the door*). You have not seen her? Miserable man, she's glorious! You can catch a glimpse through here.

JUL. (*raising his head*). No. The spell is broken — the image shattered. What strange delirium, that I should be so deceived. Oh, Thecla, pardon me! *[Buries face.*

OFF. But I tell you I don't want to see the actress. I have business with the Count of Toledo.

LAR. (*pompously*). Eh? I understand. I don't understand a word. Not want to see the greatest actress of the age? Go, miserable man! There sits the one you seek.

OFF. (*tapping his shoulder*). Count Julian of Toledo. From the King.

JUL. My passports! And an order to quit France instantly! Am I going mad? What new mystery's this?

OFF. From·Her Excellency the Marchioness of Pompadour.

[Gives paper.

JUL. (*reads*). "Count, what are you about? The Prince of Novgorod is furious, and tells the King that you or he must go.

Abrupt dismissal of an envoy means war. With every desire to aid you, I knew not what to say when the vast numbers of the Russian troops were laid before me. Our armies will start shortly for Prussia, and the Czarina would be too powerful an ally for Frederick. For the time you must be sacrificed. On the first opportunity you shall be recalled. Farewell. Antoinette de Pompadour." Mystery on mystery. Why this never-ceasing interest, which asks for no return; and yet—the riddle of the fan !

> " Unless a man can mount he ne'er will rise ;
> Timid, he 'll not win smiles from ladies' eyes."

Alas, alas ! It 's plain enough.

OFF. A carriage waits without. My orders are to see you to the frontier.

JUL. To go ! without a moment's delay. Surely I trace in this the direct finger of Fate. I thank the King ; he saves me from myself. One moment, sir, and I will follow you. (*Writes in note-book, and tears out page.*) M. Laroque ; a favour, ere I go. Deliver for me this note to Mademoiselle Fidès.

[*Applause without.*

LAR. Hark ! the curtain's down. You can yourself speak with her.

JUL. No, no ! a thousand times ! Destiny has willed it otherwise. I am ready, sir. [*Exit, hurriedly, with* OFFICER.

(*Enter, at opposite door,* MADAME DE PIERREFITTE.)

MAD. DE P. Where is the Count? Quick ! Banished, through this jade's insolence. Oh, she shall repent it bitterly.

LAR. He went but now. See (*runs to window*), his carriage drives away, surrounded by an armed escort.

MAD. DE P. Gone ! Was he downcast, or did he go in wrath?

LAR. He left quietly, confiding to me this note for Mademoiselle Fidès.

MAD. DE P. For *her!* Ah ! (*places hand on heart*) but she shall rue this day. (*Aloud, recovering herself*). A note; yes. But he also bade me send her this, which, in his hurry, he forgot. A token she will understand. (*Gives rose; takes fan from table.*) Be discreet. Not a word ! [*Exit.*

LAR. Not a word ! May I lose my important post if I comprehend a syllable !

(*Enter* THECLA.)

THEC. Not here ? And yet I saw him leave his place. Oh ! I am young again. This is more than Spring ; I feel as though I had commenced Eternity ! His words have lightened my overburdened heart.

LAR. Madame, by Count Julian's bidding I was to give you these.

THEC. My token, returned; and some written lines! Heaven! a presentiment of evil chills my joy!

LAR. (*who has been to the centre door, returns. Applause without*). Madame, the public calls for you. No wonder. You really were sublime! Hark! they clamour for you, although the act has not concluded. Come.

THEC. Let them wait. I am fatigued—have need of rest. Go and announce as much. [*Exit* LAROQUE. I dare not open it. As from Pandora's box, might not *my* happiness take to flight? Courage! (*Reads.*) "You were right. As you said, you wear the form of another, sanctified by death. The face is there; the soul bears no resemblance. I remain faithful to the memory of her who died for me. There yawns a gulf between me and the confidant of Pompadour. Farewell!" The confidant of Pompadour! Mole that thou art! Could'st thou not understand that it was for thy sake, that I might watch o'er thee? Did not thy heart see through this shallow artifice? The poor flower that once thou cravedst, now dead and withered is returned to me! Was it in scorn or ignorance? "Faithful to the memory of her who died for me." Oh, Julian! Blind, blind! I am Thecla—Thecla herself alive, who loves thee still!

[*A pause. Music as in other Tableaux.*

Enter LAROQUE.

LAR. Mademoiselle, they are impatient. Listen! They will tear up the seats.

THEC. Count Julian was here just now. Where did he go? Quick! Speak!

LAR. Count Julian! Always Count Julian! He is gone away. Listen how the public stamp and shout! I implore you, come!

THEC. Gone! Where? when?

LAR. By order of the King—at the instance of the Prince of Novgorod. Why, I know not. Oh, those poor seats! If obdurate to me, have pity, at least, on them.

THEC. Dismissed from Court, and I the innocent cause? An eoy u—war with Spain! When may we meet again? Laroque —q ick, run!

LAR. Run! Yes; to appease the angry multitude. Your waywardness will bring my hairs with sorrow to the grave. Though the position's high, who 'd try to govern theatres! [*Exit.*

THEC. Where has he gone? How to find him? The Pompadour has retired to rest.

[*Announcement without, "Make way there for the Princess of Novgorod."*

My sister! She stands high in the world's respect. She——
Enter OLIVIA.

Madame, one word.

OLIV. (*coldly*). What would Mademoiselle Fidès with me?

THEC. Oh, madame, help me! The Count of Toledo has been dismissed from Court on demand of the Prince, your husband. I am the wretched cause. Should there be war with Spain, who can tell when he may return? I have urgent need to speak with him at once. The happiness of two lives hangs upon my words. Thank me that you can help, at least, to blot out a bitter wrong.

OLIV. The actress forgets her position and mine. I regret it, but I cannot move in this. Count Julian publicly insulted my lord, for which it is just that he should suffer. Let me pass.

THEC. But I tell you that I love this man. Help me to see him. I conjure you, by your dead sister's memory.

OLIV. Nay, the amours of our tinselled queens of tragedy can hardly interest the Princess of Novgorod. Let me pass, I say, or I call the guard.

THEC. And can that name not stir your stony heart! Do you owe her nothing, this sister for whom you wear this mockery of woe? I have been told that once, in a bitter strait, she smilingly laid down her fair fame before the world for you. You accepted the life sacrifice. The time has come. Once more I charge you to repay the debt.

OLIV. Woman, you terrify me! Who are you? Are you a phantom risen from the tomb?

THEC. She gave up more than life for you. In her name I demand only that you forego a little pride! Seek out your husband; down on your knees to him; beg him, by his love for you, to bear this shock upon his vanity. Do this, and you are free. The debt is cancelled.

OLIV. Alas! he loves me not. I have no influence with him. His will is law to me. I bow and I obey. Besides, I *could* not ask this of him. The world would gibe and curl its lips at us.

THEC. The world! the world! Oh, heart of adamant! You near the bottom of the precipice. Remember the words of one who is no more—whose warning returns from the groves of eternal sleep: "When you shall stand in the solitude of death, your God shall melt away, leaving you alone 'mid the curses of your victims. And the first voice raised to denounce and to upbraid will be the voice of the idol of your hands!"

OLIV. (*agitated*). Who are you, I say, who dare to use such words to me? My sister is dead. It is better that she should be so. She disgraced her name and lineage——

THEC. (*in violent indignation*). As you've a soul to save, 'tis false!   [*Seizes her arm.*

OLIV. Help, help!

THEC. (*flings her from her*). Be not afraid. You've nought to fear from me. (*Bitterly*). The Countess Von-Thürenau is dead; may her bones rest in peace! Go on your thorny way, and, if not yet too late, think of your sister's prophecy.

OLIV. But tell me—

THEC. (*pointing off*). Go! (*Remains in an attitude of command till* OLIVIA *has slunk off, then sinks on a seat and sobs.*) She's gone—she's gone, to glide respected through the hollow world I learned early to despise. Heaven grant our paths may never cross again. The player envies not her great estate. But time moves on, bearing away my opportunity. My life has shrunk into a shrivelled scroll.

Enter VOLTAIRE.

VOL. How now, Thecla?

THEC. Your hand has helped me when I needed strength; you have encouraged me when sinking in despair. Oh! aid me now in my great extremity.

VOL. Why, child! Pale and trembling, fresh from the glories of your art; flushed with a triumph well deserved. I hoped to find you contented and serene. What's this? A reaction of spirits overstrained. Did I not warn you that it would cost you tears of blood?

THEC. No; I am well. Well! I spoke to him. He was here just now. Unwittingly he told me that he loved me still, and his wandering words spoke very truth. Oh! Voltaire, the cup I've sought so long was at my lips. When I would have drank, lo! it was dashed from me. Dear friend, there's treachery in this. Fate unaided were not so relentless. My brain reels. I feel I shall go mad.

VOL. Child, child! What is this amazing mystery of love, which sweeps reason headlong from her throne? One by one you break down my patiently raised prejudices of years.

THEC. I tell you that not half-an-hour ago he told me that he loved me still.

VOL. Count Julian—

THEC. Is fled. I must speak with him. There's agony we cannot twice endure and live. One little word and all would be set straight. Forgive my wayward speech, old friend, who've counselled me with a deep tenderness my dead father might have borne. Sole succour of my solitary life, desert me not in this my darkest hour. [*She clings to him.*

VOL. This is the fever of a distempered mind. You are ill. Your brain has been taxed too much.

THEC. The precious sand drips pitilessly on. I tell you I must speak with him or I shall die.

VOL. So far gone as this? Well, well, your hand is cold, your face on fire. There, he shall be found; he cannot yet be far, and I myself will be your courier. I cannot bring him back, but you shall go with me. Oh! prejudices of a life, that I should sink to this — *I*, the high priest and patriarch of Reason!

THEC. Thanks, thanks. I knew you'd not abandon me till I flit past all mortal help. (*She lays her head on his breast, having risen from her seat.*) Staunchest, truest friend.

VOL. And is it I who in my old age would play the benignant fairy. Oh, Nemesis! oh, Goddess of Folly! What would my grave disciples say if they could see me now?

THEC. (*still head on breast, but now coaxing him*). You will go at once. Never heed the night. Its breath is soft and warm to strengthen man against the buffets of another bitter day. There's no time to be lost. Could I but tell him all I feel, I should sink to sleep upon his breast in peace.

VOL. (*in tears*). Cease! Speak not yet of sleep. Death is for me, old useless trash that clogs the wheels of time. Rocked by the zephyrs of success, all the world has to give lies at your feet. Its sunniest rays play in your silken hair. There, there! You could always wind cross old Voltaire round your dimpled baby finger. I'll do your errand. I will seek him out, and you shall go with me to him. What is this? A tear! Pooh, the rooms are hot! Do you not feel their overpowering warmth? (*This irascibly.*) I'll speak to the Pompadour about it. The ventilation is so very bad.

[*Blows his nose violently.*

Enter LAROQUE (*applause without*).

LAR. In the name of Heaven, do you not hear? The act is over now, and they insist on seeing you. Just hearken to their rage! They cry and stamp like fiends let loose. Madame, come at once, or really there'll be damage done.

THEC. What care I for their applause since *he* is there no more?

LAR. (*in agony*). But I implore for *my* sake! They *will* tear up the seats.

THEC. Leave me in peace. Can you not see how deep my suffering is?

LAR. Oh, yes! of course. You are fatigued, and I told them so. But think of the public wrath.

THEC. Am I then a slave? See! I break my bonds (*throws off some portion of her head-dress*). I reclaim my sacred liberty—all that is left to me—a right to pine in solitude and die. I act no more! Away with these foolish trappings, which insult my grief (*tosses away bracelets, &c.*). These emblems of a false god I spurn henceforth. Art is as empty as all other things. An image fair, but as dumb and hollow as all in this fickle world. I here renounce it. May it be accursed! Voltaire, I am strong. Let us go at once.

LAR. What a scandal's here! Does the dignity of my position——

Enter 2ND OFFICER, *with soldiers.*

OFFICER. Mademoiselle Fidès, chief actress of the Comédie Française. For having failed in due respect to King and Court, I am to conduct you at once to the prison of Fort L'Évêque. Follow me.

LAR. To the common prison! Our great actress—the glory of the artistic world? There must be some mistake.

VOL. To prison—you! (*Clasps her in his arms.*) Truly fate is hard on us. Then you can't go with me. But these old bones shall learn to fly and bring you news.

THEC. (*leaning on him*). No. The struggle's past. The cruel hand of destiny forbids that he and I should meet again on earth. I see it written, and I bow my head. Grieve not for me. I have tried to live. Have I not tried, Voltaire? A waste of time and strength. I have only learned to die. (*She clings closely to him.*)

VOL. We owe all this to that wind-bag of blatant pride, the Prince of Novgorod.

Enter MADAME DE PIERREFITTE.

MAD. DE P. Not so. You owe this stroke to me. She dared, a mere adventuress, forsooth, to measure arms with a high-born lady of the Court. I said I'd grind her to her true level in the dust. I've kept my word. Remove your prisoner!

VOL. My faith in human wickedness begins to breathe again. Trust one woman to hunt another to death! [*Curtain.*

TABLEAU IV.—*Green Room, Comédie Française.*

Pictures on walls, busts, clocks; running obliquely on one side a low passage, with trap in wall.

Enter LAROQUE *and* MARTIN.

LAR. I'm worn out, bated and fussed past bearing. Though 'tis no doubt a grand post, who would willingly be ballet-inspector to the King? Talk of crowned heads and thorny pillows, indeed; it is nothing to the never-ending worry of our petty spites and jealousies behind the scenes. Now just see how awkwardly I'm placed. The performance to commence in half-an-hour; the theatre crowded with the flower of our gay capital; His Majesty (Heaven bless him!) will presently be here. And—hush—whisper, lest we be overheard—it is possible I may find myself without a heroine.

MAR. What! No chief actress! But Mademoiselle Clairon came in just now, I saw her pass; and Madame Dumesnil.

LAR. Both refuse to play the part because, forsooth, Fidès made it once her own. Oh, these women, these women! I've stormed, begged, supplicated, all in vain. I see that in the end I shall be disgraced, hurled from my pedestal, return to black-beetles and spiders, perchance! I shiver at the thought! Why could I not leave theatres alone and be content with funerals? Of course you fail to understand. The case stands thus. Count Julian returns to-day to Paris, by express order of the Pompadour, though why,—but never mind that; and, by way of delicate compliment to him as poet, she has ordered that 'Sappho' shall be played to-night. So far so good. But 'Sappho' was the sublimest creation of our poor Fidès, and in her absence none of her compeers dare undertake the character. Clairon shrugs her dimpled shoulders, Dumesnil pouts and turns away. It's as much as my place is worth to disobey the favourite; yet we can't give a tragedy with the chief character expunged. Was ever luckless man in such a strait!

MAR. Serious indeed. What do you propose to do?

LAR. If Fidès could only be induced—impossible—? Well, well. In my difficulty I have fallen back upon a *débutante*—chief pupil of the Conservatoire, who was not to have made her bow for six months at least. But there's no help for it. A Sappho of some kind we must have, and so I told the girl, in spite of tears. She is to get through Sappho somehow, and Heaven in mercy grant that she may not be hissed! But you bring news of Fidès. When may she resume her work?

MAR. With rest and care within the year, perhaps—perhaps never.

LAR. Dear doctor, what are you saying?

MAR. The truth. (LAR. *groans.*) Her health, which has been on the wane, has quite succumbed since that scandal at Versailles.

LAR. Absurd. She was detained barely through the night. Early next morning the Pompadour ordered her release.

MAR. True. Yet from that day her faculties have collapsed. She sits for hours gazing on vacancy, listless and sad, as though stunned by some violent shock. At the least sound she starts and trembles. The wear and tear of her profession has proved too much for her.

LAR. Tut, tut! You exaggerate to show off your skill. Not believing the case as bad as you report, I have written, urgently requesting her presence here.

MAR. No use; she will not come. At any rate I have given my opinion; the responsibility of action rests with you. [*Exit.*

LAR. Yes! Everything falls on me! Was ever luckless wretch so harried and tormented. Ah, M. de Voltaire!

Enter VOLTAIRE.

I'm at my wits' end. I wish that I was dead.

VOL. (*laughing at him*). Oh human nature! thou maze of contradictions! How many thousands call on death and cling to life the closer! Why bear a burthen we would be tossing on the ground? Is life *so* hard? Go buy a rope and hang yourself.

LAR. I tell you I shall be disgraced.

VOL. Oh sorrow worse than death! What are your troubles?

LAR. Without Fidès I am lost. Is there no hope? (VOL-TAIRE *shakes head.*)

Enter SERVANT.

SERV. You are wanted, sir, upon the stage.

LAR. Yes, yes, I come. Who would be stage manager!
[*Exit.*

VOL. Ha! ha! A whimsical world. One-half plays at love, while the other devours its neighbours openly!

Enter THECLA, *pale and weak, who sinks into a chair.*

VOL. You here, Thecla? Risen but now from a bed of sickness. How imprudent.

THEC. I am restless and feverish. Laroque sent for me, I know not why, and I have come—(*with bitter laugh*)—I have come to haunt the scenes of former triumphs, although I act no more. That has glided into the past—the bitter past!

VOL. Always brooding over what may never be recalled! You are still young and beautiful. Believe me, child. Turn rather to the future. Sunshine cast on the ocean of the past brings water to the eyes.

THEC. Sunshine. Yes. The sun shines on the grateful earth, which springs to infinite life in thankfulness. What have I done that the world should be wrapt in gloom for me?

VOL. (*puts hand on her head*). Child, child! who wert to have been the solace of my age. Is not this strange? I vow thou art the more aged of the two, spite of my wrinkled cheeks and shrunken limbs. Oh, Thecla, Thecla! where is the art that was to raise you above the world? Where is the friend who was to soothe your every grief? Return to the healing goddess, and seek comfort on her breast.

THEC. (*sombre*). There is no healing goddess but death! My art! What has it done for me? It has procured me insult before the man I love. It has showered tinsel flattery on me from those who clap their hands, while they secretly despise me as a mountebank. My art! Another of the many frauds of this false world. Your creed of nothingness is the true one, Voltaire, though it terrified me once, and chilled my ardent youth. (*Very sombre*). To sleep a dreamless sleep and be forgot!

VOL. We must have another doctor. Martin's drugs take no effect. You are very ill.

THEC. Then is not this your creed?

VOL. (*confused*). Yes, yes; but it sounds scarcely fitting on the lips of youth. Old Doctor Martin——

THEC. Is like all the rest. He scans the surface ailments of the body, nor dreams that the mind may have its fevers—more terrible—beyond the reach of mortal pharmacy!

VOL. Intermittent fever—of the mind; for you vary strangely. On some days you are almost yourself; on others you do naught but call on death.

THEC. The flame of faith still burns within, lighting with flickering spark the darkness of my soul; and then the waves of doubt surge over me, and all is black, without a ray of light. I took the drugs that Martin ordered me, rather than pain the kind old man, though the medicine which soothes my aching heart lies *here*.

VOL. Martin says——

THEC. That I am fading slowly away. Not so. I suffer from excess of life—repressed, neglected, beaten down. (*Draws out letter.*) See—this is his hand. "Our mysterious communion becomes my first necessity. There is a depth of poetic passion in your soul which gives me strength to bear. Happy the man whom you shall bless with love. May we never meet?" (*She sighs.*) Never more!

VOL. Then you love him still.

THEC. Yes. My love is life to me. I cling to it as a ship-wrecked mariner clings to the plank which shall bear him to a haven.

VOL. Frail is the haven, and the waves beat cruelly. Well, I give the riddle up. The day that man was born, logic was murdered. Perhaps we are both right, or perhaps but a pair of fools.

THEC. (*meditating sombrely*). To sleep and be forgot. To fight our puny fight, then crumble into dust intangible! No, Voltaire. It were too cruel. 'Tis a false creed. Love shines on us from a world beyond the stars, and points to his brother, Faith. *He* teaches that we are immortal through his own immortality. You, who are blind to Love, can you not discern the majesty of Death? As the sun sinks into the sea to rise on other climes, so is the journey of the soul into the regions of eternity. Woe to the man who knows not Love, for to him shall his angel brother veil his face.

VOL. Meanwhile, this love of which you speak has made a wreck of you. Five short years ago, who so gay as the Countess Thecla? Bright in the glitter of youth and talent, you spurned the world which lay prostrate at your feet. Then came the shadowy visitant, and you fell bowed and broken, crushed by those awful shades. You took refuge in a mimic world, illumined by the divine halo of art. Return to it, Thecla. In the splendour of your triumphs you will find, if not peace, at least forgetfulness.

THEC. My art proved as unstable as all here below. I have abandoned it for ever.

Enter LAROQUÉ *and* MARTIN.

LAR. What do I hear? Mademoiselle Fidès, if you have any mercy, withdraw those words. You have obeyed my summons. Thanks. Mademoiselle, have pity on a frantic manager, whom everybody unites to drive stark mad. Since you retired from the stage, I have not known a moment's peace. The tide of mean jealousy and spite, which your genius helped to stem, has broken loose, and the place is a Pandemonium. All the ladies claim the same part, and will have it, or they won't act at all. At one moment they are not on speaking terms, and rehearse through the medium of interpreters; at another, they rave and wrangle, and threaten one another's hair and cheeks. Come, when will you return to us? Name your own conditions.

THEC. If I wished it, doctor, when could I act again?

MAR. In your present state of weakness, through which, with care, we hope to bring you safely——

THEC. Well?

MAR. Just now, violent emotion might prove fatal to you. In six months we shall be more fit to judge.

THEC. You see, Laroque, I could not help you, even if I would. But, as I wrote to you, build no hopes on me. I tell you, finally, that I shall act no more.

LAR. Then I shall certainly revisit that prison cell. Ugh!

MAR. Now, madame, a word of advice. Lengthened conversation is injurious to you. It is late. Your carriage waits below. Let me conduct you home.

THEC. You are right. My head swims. Dear friend, give me your hand. Thanks. I am better now.

[*They place her in chair.*

VOL. Well?

MAR. (*feeling pulse*). No cause for alarm; though her pulse beats feebly.

Enter ERFURT.

ERF. Good evening, gentlemen. The house is crammed. Are you ready to begin?   [THECLA *places hands before her eyes.*

VOL. What ails you?

THEC. Nothing. 'Tis over. He brings a breath from the outer world, which I once pretended to despise, but now have learned to hate.

ERF. What! Mademoiselle Fidès? This is a joyful surprise indeed! Do you act to night?

LAR. Alas! no. (*Aside*). Mouldy bread and spiders. Ugh!

ERF. No? Ah, well! Next week, perhaps? No? Then the week after. The most dreadful rumours have been afloat concerning you. We have been positively in despair.

VOL. Has the Court energy for so violent an emotion?

ERF. You wrong the Court, which is a heaven on earth. We dance and sing, knowing that there's naught beyond the grave. Such balls!—such picnics in the park! Madame de Pierre-fitte——

THEC. (*rousing her*). Aye—what of her?

ERF. She's the centre and mainspring of our festivity—a very Euphrosyne! She expressed the deepest sorrow at your illness, madame. Indeed, we were told by her that you had caught the small-pox in prison and were dying. "I shall never forgive myself," she repeated frequently; "if, through my means, the stage is robbed of its fairest ornament."

VOL. Oh, woman, woman!

THEC. (*grinding teeth*). Did she say so—the viper!

Enter SERVANT.

SERV. This letter has just been left for Mademoiselle Fidès.

THEC. A letter !—give it me.

MAR. Take it, M. de Voltaire. At present she's not fit to read.

THEC. Give it me, I say. (*Rises, and falls back into seat.*) From him—I knew it—I felt it *here.*

MAR. I cannot authorize this. I declare——

THEC. That I am too weak to read it ? (*Smiling.*) How vain a thing is the boasted science of man ! (*Reads.*) " I feel that I must see you once again. I acted hastily. May I not have misread your message ? Yet, no—the chapter of my life was closed five years ago, and to the end I am condemned to wander on alone. Though faithful to my vows, yet must I gaze once more upon your face, which is to me a vision of the dead. I shall be in Paris for a single night on the 7th of October, and will attend the theatre in hopes of seeing you. I shall mark the genius shining from your eyes, shall wave you a farewell, and then we meet upon this earth no more.—JULIAN." What day of the month is this ?

LAR. The 7th of October.

THEC. To-night ! What piece is played ?

LAR. 'Sappho,' by express order of the Pompadour.

THEC. Sappho—my part—who plays it ?

LAR. Alas ! one who will certainly be hissed, and who is in tears at the prospect in her dressing-room.

THEC. Doctor, I have often assured you your science was vain. I will prove it to you.

MAR. How ?

THEC. You said that in six months I might possibly return to the stage.

MAR. I repeat it.

THEC. And I say that you are wrong. I shall act to-night.

MAR. Impossible !

LAR. What ! Can I believe my ears ?

THEC. Laroque, I must play Sappho to-night. On this one condition I return to you. (*Aside.*) I will crush her with my art, and he shall be mine yet.

MAR. This imprudence may cost your life. My conscience bids me prevent——

THEC. Prevent me ! Try !

VOL. (*to whom she had handed the letter*). But can you do it ? Will your strength hold out ?

THEO. I can, because I will.

LAR. I dance on air. There's not a moment to lose. Go and dress. Angel of comfort—spirit of poetry—go, while I present myself before the house, and announce the glorious news.

MAR. I most solemnly protest——

THEC. See, I am strong ; come with me.

> [*Exit with* DOCTOR ; LAROQUE *supports her out, then comes down.*]

LAR.   " On her fair brow Minerva's wisdom sits ;
        Her hair, like Venus' own, is glittering bright."

But hold ! Take care, Laroque. No more odes : they're dangerous. Yet I'm too gay for elegies. Was there ever such a piece of luck ? The Pompadour will be delighted—the sun of royalty will shine on me. But let me fly to announce the surprise we have in store.   [*Exit.*

VOL. What courage—what an iron will set in a form how frail !

ERF. (*looking about*). And so this is the celebrated green-room of the Comédie Française. Art has here a gorgeous temple, worthy of the noble priesthood who inhabit it. Portraits of artists who live on a strip of canvas, and whose memory shall endure for ages when their bodies are dust, and their genius fled with their souls into oblivion. A strange thought that, M. de Voltaire — that a few inches of flaxen fibre should be more enduring than the supreme triumph of creation, the human soul.

VOL. The world is made up of paradoxes, young man, and this is one of them. Tell me more of the doings of the Court. How I hate it and its ingratitude ! Would you believe it, they have set up Crébillon against *me*, and swear my tragedies are nothing to the soapsuds in his 'Catiline.' Oh, what an evil thing is man ; how well that he lives not beyond the grave ! I am half-persuaded to withdraw and live a hermit's life, write panegyrics on imaginary virtue, and instruct the bucolic mind on human vanity. But the Court would gladly see me go, and so I stay. The Russian Ambassador gave a ball last night ?

ERF. Yes, and the Princess of Novgorod was resplendent with icy sparkle. His Majesty led her through a dance, and swore she froze his fingers to the bone. Such rarefied virtue is too intense for our nether world.

VOL. So will it ever be. The gaudy weed spreads its flaunting petals to the air, while the healing herb shrouds its powers for good deep down among its leaves. And silly man—how blind !—grinds the second under foot, and decks with the first the tresses of the fair !

Enter LAROQUE.

LAR. I 've made the announcement, and never was there such enthusiasm. The Pompadour will certainly pay me handsomely for this. I 've told the girl upstairs, too, of her reprieve, and her tears have ceased to flow. All goes as merrily as a chime of bells.

ERF. Then I go to take my place. Master, good night. (*Kisses* VOLTAIRE's *hand.*) M. Laroque, I congratulate you. [*Exit.*

Enter SERVANT.

SERV. The Duke of Orno sends to say he must have a seat at any price.

LAR. There are none left.

SERV. His grace says that box No. 15 is still unoccupied.

LAR. It is taken.

SERV. He would know by whom.

LAR. By a messenger from the Spanish Embassy.

[*Exit* SERVANT.

Enter 2ND SERVANT.

2ND SERV. M. Diderot and the German Ambassador request seats upon the stage. The Court being present, their absence, they say, might be remarked.

LAR. The seats on the stage are taken. As it is, the performers will scarce have room to move. Good heavens! Will you leave me in peace? And now I go to await the arrival of His Majesty.

*Fausse sortie—*MARTIN *enters, and runs against him.*

MAR. Stay, M. Laroque. Once more I tell you that Mademoiselle Fidès is not fit to act. She can scarcely stand—her memory flickers—she is playing with her life.

LAR. But she says she is strong and well.

MAR. There is some secret motive for her strange behaviour. Even now, while her tirewomen are busy with their task, her head sinks upon her breast, and she starts from lethargy, murmuring through set teeth, "I can, because I will." I return to my post, and warn you that I shall endeavour to take her home. I shall do my duty—you do yours. [*Exit.*

LAR. My duty! my duty! It's very fine talking, but after the enthusiasm of just now, I dare not. What am I to do? Oh, my poor head. M. de Voltaire, why do you say nothing? Your cynical smile will drive me quite distracted.

VOL. Never fear; Fidès will recite. When she says she *will*, you may safely trust in her. See—here she is.

[*Fidès appears as Sappho—they help her down.*

LAR. How do you feel, my dearest friend? Rest in this chair. Would you like something — a glass of water with a little cordial in it?

THEC. Thanks, no. I am well. Quite well. A blessed calm has settled on my breast.

VOL. Was not my counsel wise — to seek the soothing goddess, Art. But do not overtax your strength. The doctor said——

THEO. That I was feverish, though I told him my spirit was at peace. Poor human science! Feverish—yes! What actor but burns with fever whilst portraying the immortal woes made sacred through the genius of our poets? What is our enthusiasm but fever? The fever of Art—the fever of creation. Do you think that I could rise to the last act of Sappho were I not torn by passion—which is fever? Do you think——

LAR. We will think anything you please, if you will not agitate yourself. You require calm and rest.

THEO. You are right. See how obedient I am, and in what perfect peace! (*Coaxing him.*) Come here, Laroque. Sit on this stool beside me. Tell me—who is there in the house?

LAR. Who? Two thousand people, at least.

THEC. (*impatient*). Yes, yes. That is not what I ask. Who is there—of importance?

LAR. The whole flower of the Court. The King (Heaven bless him!) will presently be here.

THEO. No, no. I mean not him.

LAR. Oh! Among the literary world——

[*All this time* VOLTAIRE *is sitting by, laughing.*

THEO. Well?

LAR. There's Crébillon, and Holbach——

THEC. (*pettishly*). I care not for them.

LAR. An illustrious stranger arrived last night. He, too, will honour us.

THEC. (*joyously*). Yes? His name?

LAR. His Majesty's father-in-law—King Stanislas of Poland.

THEC. (*relapsing*). What are kings to me? No one else?

LAR. No one.

THEC. Thank you, Laroque.

VOL. My child, are you certain of your memory? Were it not prudent to study your part awhile?

Enter SERVANT.

SERV. Sir, you are wanted on the stage.

LAR. I come. They never give me a moment's peace.

[*Exit with* SERVANT.

Vol. Do you know, Thecla, that you have taught me something—me, the philosopher? All is so grovelling here below, it is well something higher should exist, if only in the imagination. Your eyes are bright—you are better already. Truly art is the real life, and the red rag fame is not without its worth.

Thec. I sought fame, never for myself, always for him. I will say to him one day—Julian, Thecla and Fidès are but one. For love of you one died, the other sprang to life. For you alone I became famous. Would you have love and sacrifice, love's offspring? See, these garlands of applause, of admiration, that I gathered but for you. You care not for them? Behold, I cast them all away—I renounce them every one—for *you !*

Vol. Thecla, your hand trembles——

Thec. (*sinking*). Oh, if he were not to come! If the only strand that binds me yet to life were now to snap and leave me anchorless!

Vol. But he *will* come—his letter tells you so. For mercy's sake do not torment yourself. He may be there now; Laroque may not have seen him.

Thec. True, dear friend, always my help in trouble. In the passage yonder is an opening, through which you may survey the house.

Vol. I understand.

Theo. (*takes his hand*). Thanks. I will look over my part— give it me.

> " What is this shade that like a phantom sits
> 'Twixt me and light of day?
> I neither hate nor fear thee, Alceon,
> Nor yet can I love thee."

Well, Voltaire?

Vol. He has not yet come.

Theo. Not come? (*Sinks back.*)

Vol. Stay.

Thec. Is it he?

Vol. No ; but there is a box vacant.

Thec. His, perchance.

Vol. The door opens.

Theo. It is he!

Vol. The figure stands in shadow—I cannot discern.

Thec. Oh, look again!

Vol. He comes forward—yes, Count Julian of Toledo.

Thec. (*rises*). At last ! Let my eyes rest on him. Julian, my Julian, how sad and worn. Now I can be great. To-night

I shall excel myself.   His Sappho shall speak thrilling words to him through me.*

Vol. Child, you are transfigured.   Only speak presently as you spoke just now, and you will be sublime.

Thec. My head swims; my mind flutters beyond my grasp. Hear me through my part, dear friend.   My memory must not fail me now.

Vol. Give me the book.   Let us begin where you hurl your scorn at Alceon.   He says—where is it—here,—"Ah, you turn pale."

Thec. "Not so, Alceon.   You quail beneath my steady gaze. I place my trust——"

Vol. "In Him?"

Thec. "In my own strength.   I have looked falsehood in the face.   The monster shrunk—spread her foul wings, and fled, baffled, out of sight."

Vol. Brava! brava!   Come a little forward, when Alceon says, "I hate thee, Sappho!"

Thec. (coming forward). "Mine eyes gush forth for thee."

Vol. "Away with pity.   I will none of it."

Theo. "My hate thou ne'er shalt have, whate'er befall.   The snake lies crushed beneath my feet.   Spite of my wrongs, I conquer, and with a smile I pass."

Vol. Brava!   What a gesture!—what a look!   Were I the author of the tragedy, I could desire no more.   Let us go on.

Thec. I dare not.   As the scene proceeds, I have need of all my strength.   My heart and voice must swell with the cadence of despair.   Mocked and despised before all Greece!   Yet what was Greece to her?   Spurned before him in whose affection alone she lived, as I live in Julian's.   There lay the agony. Poor Sappho!   what desperate anguish have I to delineate!—and justly to portray must delve into my own heart's memories.   Let me try the first speech.   The high priest says——   What says he?

Vol. "Go, fallen priestess, go.   Thou art accursed!
          Wander away, alone, exiled, disgraced,
          Far from the haunts of men."

Thec. (rising to the situation gradually).
    "Nay; hallowed by Love, I tower above ye all!
    Approach if thou darest, Alceon!
    Advance one step ye cannot—ye are webbed in magic spells!
    Who from my hands shall wrest the sacred lyre?

---

* These sentences, apparently long, are to bring her down from the back, slowly, to which she had rushed.

It is mine.　Its mystic chords baptised
With my soul's tears.　Back ! back, I say !
Ye *shall* not tear my treasure from me !"

      [*Soft music of stringed instruments—she plays lyre.*

Through thee, poor harp, my grief finds utterance.

  " With bitter pain my bosom welleth o'er,
    With soothing dew my eyes are bathed no more,
           I bleed and sing.

    Oh, kindly death, upon whose gentle breast
    They who have fall'n in the world's fight may rest,
(*With energy.*)   Thy comfort bring.

    Mark well the world !　Idol whose scorching smile
    And murderous kiss to chasms dread beguile,
           Behold and see !

    'Mid blood and smoking holocausts he stands,
    I, too, his victim, slain by cruel hands,
(*With anger.*)   Oh, pity me !

    'Neath his destroying car must all bow down,
    Prepared to sacrifice before his frown
           Hope, Faith, and Love ?

    Sisters star-crowned, sent down amid our strife
    To whisper of another, better life
           In Heaven above.

    Who knows not Love, unworthy is to live—
    Through Him I breathe who happiness can give ;
           Or if that I

    Be doomed to perish by celestial fire,
    I, mounting radiant to my glorious pyre,
           Rejoice to die !"

      [*She totters, and falls into* VOLTAIRE'S *arms.*

VOL. Thecla, what is this—a deadly pallor spreads upon your brow ?

THEC. (*sinking into seat*). No, no.　It is nothing—I am strong.　(*Murmurs dreamily*) " To my glorious pyre—Rejoice to die."

VOL. Her great emotion's killing her.　Quick—some one—help !

LAR. (*entering*). His Majesty's arrived.　A splendid house ! I've ordered up the curtain.　All's ready to begin.　What's this ? Mademoiselle Fidès fainted when she should be on the stage ? Ill luck pursues me.　Oh, my distracted brain !　Ah !　Here's the doctor.　This is opportune.

Enter MARTIN.

MAR. (*kneeling by her — after a pause*). As I expected. Silence.

VOL. A passing faintness, doctor, is it not?

MAR. She may rally; yet, in her weakened state——

VOL. You confess, then, that your drugs are vain?

MAR. She might with care have been herself after a time; but now——

VOL. Then we'll try the last desperate remedy. There is a medicine which may save her yet. I'll wear wings upon my shrunken heels and fly. Strange that Voltaire should come to be love's messenger. [*Exit hurriedly.*

LAR. When I announced that Fidès was to act, His Majesty (Heaven bless him!) deigned graciously to touch my hand. And, now, what is to become of me? Mademoiselle, for my sake rouse yourself. Oh, doctor, if you can revive her I will give you gold.

MAR. Her life is beyond my healing art. Hope and wait.

LAR. Try something, I implore you.

THEO. (*reviving*). How bright the lamps—how great a crowd! He is there—I see him—my own Julian—I love thee. My sister, too, she of the stony heart. Hark! how they applaud. Fidès, the great actress, holds them in her thrall. "Hallowed by love, I tower above ye all! Approach if thou darest, Alceon." Stay! Do you not see him—there. He rises from his seat— glides along the corridor—now he crosses the threshold of the stage—advancing ever. The door opens—he is here——

At this moment enter JULIAN *and* VOLTAIRE. *She falls into* JULIAN'S *arms.*

JUL. Thecla!

THEC. (*laughing hysterically*). You hear him. He knows me now! Yes, Julian. For ever thine. A pall drops between me and thee. Where art thou?

MAR. 'Tis as I thought. We may expect the worst.

JUL. Thecla! Hearken! 'Tis I who speaks — thy Julian. Heaven, she hears me not. Thecla!

THEO. What is this? Not death? Oh, no. Now thou art mine once more I feel that life is beautiful. Together we will wander far away, mid purling brooks and gently waving trees. All fades dimly into night. 'Tis death indeed; but beyond the day breaks where we shall meet again, never to part through all eternity. Here is the rose you begged for once—like me, faded and withered now. Keep it; for my sake look on it sometimes.

JUL. Thecla, my love, art thou then lost to me?

THEO. Not lost. I shall be with thee still. Love never dies. Voltaire, give me thy hand; trusty friend, farewell! Where art thou, Julian? Alas! I see thee not. With my head pillowed on thy breast, tell me, ere I sleep, that thou lov'st me still— Despite the World.

JUL. I love thee—I love thee; but thou shalt not go. Thou saidst we should wander in far-off lands.

MAR. She's gone to a far-off land indeed!

JUL. ⎫
VOL. ⎬ Dead?

MAR. Dead!

Curtain slowly.

THE END.

LONDON: PRINTED BY
EDWARD J. FRANCIS, TOOK'S COURT,
CHANCERY LANE, E.C.

DESPITE THE WORLD:

A new Romantic Play,

IN TWO PARTS AND FOUR TABLEAUX.

BY

THE HON. LEWIS WINGFIELD

AND

GENEVIEVE DE GUERBEL.

PART I. BERLIN AND SANS SOUCI, 1746.

PART II. VERSAILLES AND PARIS, 1751.

For certain Portions of the Plot the Author is indebted to an Italian Work.

LONDON:

PRINTED BY E. J. FRANCIS, TOOK'S COURT, E.C.

1874.